ATTACHMENT AND LOSS IN CHILD AND FAMILY SOCIAL WORK

Attachment and Loss in Child and Family Social Work

Edited by
DAVID HOWE
University of East Anglia
Norwich

Ashgate

Aldershot • Brookfield USA • Singapore • Sydney

Published by
Ashgate Publishing Company
Gower House
Croft Road
Aldershot, Hants
GU11 3HR
England

Ashgate Publishing Company
Old Post Road
Brookfield
Vermont 05036
USA

Ashgate website:http://www.ashgate.com

Reprinted 1997, 1998, 1999

British Library Cataloguing in Publication Data
Attachment and loss in child and family social work
     1. Social work with children 2. Family social work
     3. Attachment behaviour in children 4. Loss
     (Psychology) in children
     I. Howe, David, 1946–
     362.7

Library of Congress Catalog Card Number: 95-83845

ISBN 1 85972 214 8

Printed in Great Britain by Biddles Limited,
Guildford and King's Lynn

Contents

Contributors

Dr Gwyneth Boswell is a Lecturer in Probation Practice in the School of Social Work at the University of East Anglia. She has been a Probation Officer and Senior Probation Officer and has researched and written widely on both violent young offenders and the Probation Service.

Marian Brandon is a Lecturer in Social Work at the University of East Anglia. She is currently researching 'significant harm' and the Children Act 1989.

Diana Hinings is a Lecturer in Social Work at the University of East Anglia. Her interests include the application of psychosocial theory to child welfare practice.

Dr David Howe is a Professor in the School of Social Work at the University of East Anglia and Editor of the journal *Child and Family Social Work*. He is the author of a number of books including most recently *On Being a Client: Understanding the Process of Counselling and Psychotherapy* (Sage 1993) and *Attachment Theory for Social Work Practice* (Macmillan 1995).

Kate Pearson is an Adoption Adviser and Senior Practitioner for Essex Social Services Department.

Stephen Parvez Rashid entered social work in 1968 and qualified in 1973. After local authority experience as a social worker and team leader, he was appointed Lecturer in Social Work at the University of East Anglia in 1980. His interests include anti-racist social work and mental health. He is currently Co-Director of a research project on the placement of black children.

Gillian Schofield is a Lecturer in Social Work at the University of East Anglia. She is an experienced Guardian ad Litem and the author of *The Youngest Mothers* (Avebury 1994).

Dr June Thoburn is a Professor in the School of Social Work at the University of East Anglia. She has undertaken several research studies on family placement for children in care and is frequently asked to be a witness in contested adoption cases.

Peter Wedge is Professor of Social Work and Dean of the School of Health and Social Work at the University of East Anglia. His research interests include child development, services to children and aspects of penal policy and practice.

Acknowledgements

This book is based on papers given at a Conference held in Southwold in early January 1995. The Conference was in part supported by a grant from the Central Council for the Education and Training of Social Workers who were keen to encourage links between research, theory and practice in the field of child and family social work. The authors are extremely grateful for CCETSW's support and sponsorship.

1 Attachment theory in child and family social work

David Howe

Human beings are social beings. If we are to be socially competent and reasonably able to handle relationships, it is important to understand how we become adequate social beings. Indeed, if we fail to act appropriately or effectively in our day-to-day dealings with other people, our behaviour is judged to be of social concern. This is particularly true in those areas of life to do with the rearing of children and the generation of new, sound and healthy citizens. Therefore, the quality of parenting and social abilities of children concern politicians, legislators and welfare agents.

It ought, therefore, to come as no surprise to find that a developmental perspective wedded to the practice of child and family social work produces a particularly energetic and apposite theoretical outlook. Attachment theory, which has evolved into both an elegant and eloquent view of human relationships, is one developmentally orientated psychology which continues to have an intellectual as well as a practical appeal to social workers. The theory is particularly interested in the relationship between personality development, interpersonal behaviour and the quality of the social environment during childhood. The developmental need to be in close relationships throughout childhood means that the quality of those relationships has a deep and long-lasting impact on personality and people's style of interpersonal behaviour. Adverse social relationships during childhood can affect a person's sense of well-being and self-worth, ability to form satisfying and conflict-free intimate relationships, and confidence and competence as a parent. Child and family social work considers people's present needs as well as their long-term behavioural and relationship prospects.

The chapters in this book indicate the range and depth of thinking that developmental theories can offer social workers. Like all good theories, they help practitioners (i) describe, understand and make sense of what is going on; (ii) anticipate people's future behaviours and actions; and (iii) decide what to do and how to do it. This opening chapter outlines the nature of attachment theory and introduces the five main patterns of attachment behaviour and their influence on relationships in both the lives of children and adults.

Personality formation and the development of social understanding

Our social development takes place within relationships. Many aspects of our personality and emotional make-up form during childhood as we relate with those around us. And at an even deeper level, our very concept of self emerges as we strive to make sense of other people and the relationships we have with them. In short, personality forms as social understanding develops.

This line of thought also means that the quality of relationships with other people during childhood has a direct bearing on the development of personality and the emotional make-up of the individual. The poorer the quality of people's relationship history the less robust will be their psychological make-up. Similarly, those who have experienced serious adversities during childhood will often be less confident and less competent in dealing with social relationships. Rutter (1991: 341 and 361) sums up present thinking saying that:

> . . . it seems that the postulate that a lack of continuity in the loving committed parent–child relationships is central has received substantial support . . . What has stood the test of time most of all has been the proposition that the qualities of parent–child relationships constitute a central aspect of parenting, that the development of social relationships occupies a crucial role in personality growth, and that abnormalities in relationships are important in many types of psychopathology.

In the majority of cases, the child's mother provides the most intense social and emotional experience, but the net of intimacy often extends to include fathers, older brothers and sisters, grandparents, and others. Personality and relationships are therefore linked in the following three ways:

i   individual personalities form in a matrix of close social relationships;
ii   the types of personalities which form depend in part on the quality of those social relationships, and;
iii the way different personalities handle and develop current relationships is in large measure a product of their past relationship experiences.

The importance that inherited characteristics play in personality formation and development also has to be acknowledged. There is little doubt that individuals bring to the social world a number of inborn traits. These include such things as innate cheerfulness, optimism, a tendency to be introverted or extroverted, a good sense of humour, argumentativeness, shyness, a low threshold of arousal and a high threshold of arousal. The type of social environment in which children find themselves will affect these natural temperaments every bit as much as these innate predispositions will affect the responses of other people. Strict, rigid parents may dampen the natural buoyancy of a child. But it might also be the case that a good humoured child who smiles a great deal induces warmth and laughter in those around her.

These observations remind us that psychological development takes place within a complex dynamic between nature and nurture, between an individual's genes and his or her cultural environment. Estimates suggest that genetic influences account for anything between 30 and 70% of the variation between individuals, although there is growing evidence that the higher figures may be nearer the truth.

Relationships and the quality of experience within relationships are therefore of the utmost interest and relevance to social workers involved with children and their families. What is said and done between parents affects children; the way mothers and fathers relate to their children can have a profound impact on their behaviour and development. Whether parents cooperate or quarrel, whether a mother is loving or rejecting, whether a sister is preferred or not, matters to the developing child. The parents' own history of relationships – in childhood, throughout adolescence, and during adulthood – can also help practitioners understand the quality of relationships they have with each other, their children, and officials, including social workers. Parents and their personalities produce the social environments within which their children develop.

It is the ability to understand what is happening in families in which relationships are turbulent and complex that allows practitioners to keep their thoughts clear and their emotions engaged but steady (Howe and Hinings 1995). Attachment theory emerged out of John Bowlby's highly original synthesis of developmental psychology and ecology (Bowlby 1961, 1973, 1979, 1980). His ideas captured a number of important psychological and developmental concepts under one theoretical umbrella. The recognition that relationships play a fundamental part in our understanding of personality formation, emotional development and the conduct of interpersonal behaviour meant that the psychology of the individual could no longer be understood independent of the social context. The quality of the social environment has to be understood if the individual's psychological development is to make sense. Bowlby (1984: 27–28) himself offered the following definition of attachment theory:

What, for convenience, I am terming attachment theory is a way of conceptualizing the propensity of human beings to make strong affectional bonds to particular others and of explaining the many forms of emotional distress and personality disturbance, including anxiety, anger, depression, and emotional detachment, to which unwilling separation and loss give rise . . .

3

Briefly put, attachment behaviour is conceived of any form of behaviour that results in a person attaining or retaining proximity to some other differentiated and preferred individual, who is usually conceived as stronger and/or wiser. While especially evident during early childhood, attachment behaviour is held to characterize human beings from the cradle to the grave ... The particular patterns of attachment behaviour shown by an individual turn partly on his present age, sex, and circumstances and partly on the experiences he or she has had with attachment figures earlier in his or her life.

Becoming a social being

In terms of development, there are two good reasons why being in relationship with other people is important. The human infant is particularly helpless and vulnerable as a baby. Any mechanism that ensures that the young child stays in relationship with a strong, capable, protective and interested older person increases his or her chances of survival. And secondly, developing children need to be in close relationship with at least one socially well-versed person if they are to become socially competent themselves. To be a human being is to be a social being. Everyday life is a matter of understanding and negotiating the world of other people. The more children are able to make sense of the particular social world in which they find themselves and understand their own place within it, the more adept, skilled and relaxed they can be in social relationships. In turn, this improves their chances of developing mutually rewarding friendships, entering reciprocally based intimate relationships, and becoming caring parents.

The argument is that if human beings are social beings, the ways in which we become socially competent are of great relevance to those who work with parents and their children. To be socially competent, children must develop social understanding. They must have some ideas about other people's beliefs, feelings, intentions, emotional states, desires and needs. Such understanding and empathy arise as infants enter into relationships. As children develop, they begin to learn about themselves at the same time they begin to understand other people.

Some psychologists suggest that to help us understand other people and establish relationships with them we develop a 'theory of other minds'. Children recognise that there are links between what a person thinks and feels and what he or she does. As they attribute mental states to those around them they begin to recognise that other people's behaviour can only be understood with reference to what is going on in their minds. If children are to form effective relationships, their own behaviour as well as that of other people needs to make sense. Having a theory of other minds helps children make sense of social and psychological events. It allows them to develop social understanding.

From the very beginning, babies are active participants in the busy social world in which they find themselves. They show an intense interest in people. Reciprocal relationships are a particular source of pleasure and stimulation. As soon as we are born, we are biologically predisposed to engage in social interaction. If babies are to survive and negotiate family life, they need quickly to learn how to behave in a socially intelligible manner.

Frith (1989: 169) also reminds us that 'The ability to make sense of other people is also the ability to make sense of one's self.' Children learn about their own psychological states within relationships. The more sensitive, empathic and reciprocal the communication within relationships, the more fully will children learn to understand the nature and effect of their own mental states on themselves and those around them. And the more they can understand the basis of their own thoughts and feelings, the more skilled will they become at understanding and interacting with other people. Children who develop good social empathy are not only more skilled in relationships they are also more co-operative, considerate and compassionate.

Internal working models

Different types of personality hint at the different ways in which people have tried to make sense of and adjust to their relationship environment. Adverse environments which lack love, mutuality and empathy are less conducive to the formation of secure and confident personalities. The coherence of people's cognitive organisation reveals the type of psychological adjustments which they have had to make in order to cope with their social environment. The models used to represent relationships gradually become internalised forming the basis of personality. The individual's personality is judged by the characteristic ways in which he or she makes sense of and handles social relationships. In our development, what is on the social outside therefore establishes itself on the psychological inside. In this sense, external relationships become mentally internalised (Howe 1995: 24).

In their struggle to understand what is happening around them, babies create mental models and cognitive structures to interpret the otherwise undifferentiated din of experience. These 'internal working models' help babies make sense of what is happening around them. And once established, these models act as templates within which subsequent experiences of that type are interpreted. Of particular importance is the infant's ability to understand the relationship she has with her prime caregiver. As well as supplying comfort and safety, the attachment figure (in the first instance, usually the mother) also provides the child with his or her first opportunity to be in a relationship. To be an effective partner in the relationship, the child needs to make sense of the attachment figure both psychologically and socially. The infant needs to be able to influence her. In order to do these things, she has to build

5

up an internal working model of the mother so that her actions, feelings, beliefs and intentions can be read. Here are the beginnings of social understanding. In secure attachments, the relationship is very much a two-way affair. Each partner is aware of, interested in and alert to the other's perspective. There is 'behavioural synchrony'. The more open, full and accurate the communication between mother and child, the more the child learns to understand the mother, her own self and the relationship between them. Such mutuality encourages reciprocity, empathy, responsiveness, co-operation, regard and respect. Experience helps generate the models and the mental models then aid in the interpretation of future experience. In this way, past experiences, of which the brain has attempted to make sense, influence the way in which present experiences are approached and understood. And within this process of making sense, the infant's concept of self emerges.

Inconsistencies and distortions in the caregiver–child relationship mean that the infant's attempts to model interpersonal experience are more difficult to achieve. Not being able to make consistent or coherent sense of experience is confusing and stressful. This produces feelings of anxiety. Infants in relationship with attachment figures whose responses are unpredictable or insensitive find it difficult to develop an organised view of those figures. Without reliable internal representations, they find it difficult to read the world of other people and relationships with any degree of consistency or accuracy. Nor are they very good at predicting the consequences of their own behaviour. Finding the interpersonal world unpredictable, children are less able to act and react socially either appropriately or effectively.

Attachment behaviour

Attachment behaviour is a biological response designed to get children get into close, protective relationships. According to Bowlby (1973), the need to be close to a parent-figure and to seek love and attention is on a par with other 'primary motivational systems' including the need for warmth, food and sex. Being in close relationship ensures that infants receive protection and are provided with opportunities to develop language, social understanding and interpersonal competence. By the time they are one year old, most children have developed strong selective attachments. In most cases, these attachments are to mothers and fathers.

Attachment behaviour occurs when the child experiences anxiety or stress. Such feelings arise when the child is hungry, ill, in pain, threatened or frightened. One of the most stressful experiences for a child is the loss or fear of loss of his or her attachment figure. When anxiety levels rise, attachment behaviour is triggered. Attachment behaviour involves the child (i) seeking to get close to his or her parents to be within protective range, and (ii) experiencing parents as a 'secure base' – a place of safety and comfort from which to explore the environment. Loss or the threatened loss of the attachment figure brings about a 'separation protest'. This is an attempt on the child's part to prevent the separation or to bring about the return of the prime caregiver.

When anxiety levels are low, the child is free to explore the environment of other people and things. Children who feel secure can devote more of their time and energy to learn about people, relationships and the physical world. The more they learn and understand, the more effective they become when dealing with people and situations. And the more effective and competent they are, the more confident they feel. A benign circle sets in raising feelings of self-worth.

There is a natural tension between the need to feel secure and the need to explore. On the one hand, independence and inquisitiveness encourage learning, understanding and competence. On the other, protection means that the child lives to learn another day. Anxiety promotes attachment behaviour, but attachment behaviour inhibits exploration. Too much anxiety in a child's life therefore interferes with the ability to become effective and confident in dealing with people and situations. Securely attached children talk, play and explore more when their mothers are present. They show greater independence. Insecurely attached children are less relaxed even when their mothers are present. They play less and do not interact so readily with their peers.

Loss, anxiety, separation and the defense mechanisms

In itself, anxiety is an adaptive evolutionary response. When the individual feels threatened or distressed, the level of anxiety rises. Normally this provokes some pattern of behaviour, such as the proximity seeking response of attachment behaviour, whose aim is to protect the individual either physically or psychologically. When we are anxious, we make demands on those to whom we are closest. This reaction is most pronounced during childhood, but it is behaviour that remains active throughout adult life.

For the child, one of the most distressing experiences is to be separated from or lose one's attachment figure. Most young children react to separation by first protesting vigorously, often crying inconsolably. If the separation is prolonged (say a long stay in hospital without the child being allowed to visit), the child enters a stage in which she becomes withdrawn. She might become listless and apathetic. Little interest in shown in people or toys. Further continuation of the separation results in a final phase in which the child appears somewhat detached. There is a return to play and activity but the child lacks a sense of commitment. Life is lived but the sparkle is missing. Upon eventual reunion with the attachment figure, there is a mixture of crying, clinging, anger and even the odd burst of rejection before things gradually return to normal.

Loss is endemic in human experience. The feelings of anxiety associated with loss have their origins in childhood attachment experiences. The more traumatic the loss, the more pronounced is the anxiety and the grief reaction. Generally, though, the more secure an individual's own attachment experience during childhood, the more likely it is that he or she will adjust to the loss.

Thus, one of the most fundamental and painful experiences for the developing child to handle is the loss of the attachment figure. 'Loss', in fact, can mean a number of different things. The parent can literally be lost, say through death or abandonment. There are children who lose their parent's love and interest. These children can feel rejected. They experience hostility or abuse. Some children lose 'parts' of their parents. Mothers who are inconsistent in their care and attention provide love which is erratic and unpredictable. The result is caregiving which is incompetent and neglectful.

Each of these 'loss' experiences provokes feelings of anxiety in the child. However, loss and anxiety associated with the attachment relationship itself produces a unique set of emotional difficulties. A double blow is inflicted. The child loses the attachment figure which raises feelings of insecurity. Normally, when levels of anxiety and feelings of insecurity rise, the child increases his or her attachment behaviour. But the attachment figure's behaviour is the cause of the raised anxiety. The child suffers a conflict. The parent is either physically absent, emotionally unavailable or interpersonally inconsistent and unreliable. The child is left experiencing the full impact of the anxiety on her own. There is no secure, loving person to whom to go for comfort and safety. This combination of separation from the selective attachment figure and lack of a warm and comforting caregiver during the separation produces considerable distress.

Anxiety which cannot be reduced by attachment behaviour still has to be dealt with psychologically. Ways of trying to adjust to anxiety are known as the defence mechanisms and we all use them when we are upset and distressed. Children's feelings of fear and anger at the loss of the attachment figure are very difficult for the young mind to handle. Defence mechanisms help children cope with these disturbed and confusing feelings. If the attachment figure is the cause of the anxiety, children will simultaneously experience yearning for and anger with their caregiver. Emotionally they will want to be close to their attachment figure and yet at the same time they will want to be rid of him or her because that person is also the cause of the pain and hurt.

Patterns of attachment behaviour

Children can find themselves in one of a number of basic types of relationship experience with their selective attachment figure(s). The types vary depending on the physical and emotional (i) availability, (ii) sensitivity, (iii) reliability, (iv) predictability, and (v) responsiveness of the parent. Children who experience their parents as physically and emotionally available and responsive feel secure. The less available and responsive the parents, the more insecure will their children feel.

Each type of emotional relationship leads to a different pattern of attachment. These patterns are laid down throughout childhood. If children remain in the same relationship environment throughout their young lives, these attachment experiences continue to influence their behaviour and relationship style through into adulthood. Attachment theory helps explain adult behaviour and relationships as well as those of children. These 'continuities' of attachment patterns across the life cycle offer powerful analytical insights into the quality of relationships between partners and between parents and their children (for example, see Howe 1995).

A basic classification of attachment behaviour was developed by Mary Ainsworth who had earlier worked with John Bowlby in his first formulations of attachment theory (Ainsworth et al. 1978). Other workers have extended Ainsworth's original classification (for example, see Main and Cassidy 1988). Basically, we can identify five types of attachment experience. Each one requires the child to develop a particular type of psychological adjustment if he or she is to cope with the sort of anxieties generated in that attachment relationship. In turn, each pattern of attachment produces a broad type of personality, modified by the natural temperamental differences we all bring to relationships. The reminder is that many aspects of our personality emerge out of our relationship history. The quality of our relationship environment is in large part influenced by our attachment experiences with our prime caregivers. Therefore, the different patterns of attachment lead to different behaviours, personalities and relationship styles. The five types of attachment experience are:

1   Secure attachments.
2   Insecure, anxious and ambivalent attachments.
3   Insecure, anxious and avoidant attachments.
4   Insecure, anxious and disorganised attachments.
5   Nonattachments.

Secure attachments

Within this attachment pattern, parental care, overall, is loving, responsive and consistent. Mothers are alert and sensitive to the needs of their children. Communication between parents and children is rich and full, reciprocal and accurate, synchronous and harmonious. This allows children to establish a clear understanding of themselves, other people and the relationship they have together. A coherent and well-integrated sense of self therefore builds up within secure, two-way, caring relationships. Children develop a sense of

9

trust in the love, availability and helpfulness of their caregivers. They show some distress when they are separated, but on reunion they are warmly acknowledged and comforted and soon settle. Within secure relationships, children learn to see themselves as lovable and others as responsive and trustworthy. This promotes a sense of potency and self-worth and a personality type generally regarded as positive, socially competent and likeable. Few parents live up to the full paragon of all these virtues, but most provide, in Winnicott's (1965) splendid phrase, 'good-enough' parenting.

Secure individuals are able to form close, intimate and stable relationships in which they can give love as well as receive it. Within relationships with other people, there is humour, self-disclosure and a degree of 'connectedness.' They can cope with moderate levels of conflict, stress and frustration without resorting to disturbed or socially inept behaviour. Compared to insecure individuals, those who have enjoyed secure attachment experiences can sustain problem-solving activities for longer periods. Individuals possess self-confidence and have a reasonably positive self-image. Social relationships are handled competently and in a relaxed, trusting manner. Setbacks do not seriously upset the overall level of self-assuredness. These are 'autonomous-secure' individuals who are able to appraise themselves, their past, other people and the relationships they have with them fairly accurately and realistically (Main 1994).

Insecure, anxious and ambivalent attachments

In this category, parental care tends to be inconsistent, unreliable and unpredictable. It is not so much that mothers or fathers are unloving, rather it is that their care is erratic and insensitive. They seem unable to put themselves into their children's shoes. Communication can be disjointed. Children's signals are not always observed or read correctly. There is a lack of synchrony between parent and child. Misinterpretation and misunderstanding are more common. When children want their parent's interest, they may be ignored. But when children are playing contentedly, mothers, for example, may intrude and impose their ideas and preferences on what the children are doing. Children feel unable to communicate their emotional and cognitive state to their caregivers. Psychological boundaries and a sense of a clear, autonomous self are lacking as others seem able to intrude and define the children's experience. The behaviour of the children, not being read accurately by the caregivers, fails to bring about regular or predictable responses. As a result, children do not feel entirely in control of or able to influence the content of their relationships with others. Sometimes love and attention arrive, but just as likely they do not. This produces a fretful, continuous kind of anxiety. The fractiousness represents an attempt to try and keep the parent close by and involved.

If children suffer brief separations from their attachment figures, they exhibit considerable distress. They are very difficult to calm down upon reunion. They cling to the parent and fight them at the same time. These children are both anxious to be re-united and cross with the caregiver for causing them pain. *Ambivalent* children both demand parental attention and angrily *resist* it at the same time. They can never quite trust their parents. The fear of separation or being abandoned is ever-present. Threats of abandonment or a perceived loss of interest by the parent increase the level of distress. The anxiety this generates absorbs a lot of the children's emotional energies and deprives them of opportunities to explore the world around them in an active and confident manner. Displays of ambivalence – need and anger, dependence and resistance – is the key characteristic of this type of insecure personality.

Insensitive care and unreliable attention mean that children begin to experience themselves as ineffective in securing the love and interest of other people. This may mean, in their eyes, that they are unworthy of love and therefore unlovable. Such feelings reduce self-esteem and self-confidence.

In adolescence and adult life, the need for closeness is still keenly present, but their availability and reliability cannot be trusted or taken for granted. Relationships are sought but they provoke feelings of ambivalence and conflict: 'I need you, but I can't trust you. You may abandon me and hurt me.' The result is conflict, jealousy and possessiveness. But equally likely is the threat of walking out on the relationship as anxiety and anger mount in parallel with growing feelings of need and dependence. The ambivalent personality is racked by a deep sense of insecurity. There is a fear of letting go of relationships. People cling and hang on. The result is a constant round of threats, desperate pleas, arguments and excessive apologising and making-up. Conflict (underscored by the ambivalence that all close relationships engender) is the main relationship style. Such individuals remain *preoccupied* with both past and present relationships. There is a general confusion and muddle when relationships are discussed and evaluated (Main 1994; Howe 1995: 173–74).

The ambivalent personality is attention-seeking. Only when things are happening do individuals feel that they are engaged and involved. Feelings are acted out. Action is an attempt to ward off the fear and the anxiety of being abandoned and alone. Drama seems to be an ever-present feature in the lives of the insecure and ambivalent personality. Social workers will hear of heated rows taking place at the doctor's. Husbands will have violent quarrels with their wives suspecting them of flirting with all and sundry, even though the women are tied to the house with four young, noisy, difficult children. Not to be active, demonstrative, giving or paying attention feels like a lack of interest and rejection. In this sense, ambivalent personalities feel that people are either for them or against them, all giving or all denying. Social workers can easily be sucked into the turbulent lives of such families and drawn into the conflictual relationships which bedevil all dealings with ambivalent personality types (see Mattinson and Sinclair 1979 for a good account of such families known to a social services department).

Insecure, anxious and avoidant attachments

Avoidant attachments arise when parents are indifferent towards or even rejecting of their children. They show a lack of interest in or concern with their children's needs and emotional states. Unlike the parents of ambivalent children, there is a perverse kind of consistency in their relationship style which tends to be uniformly neutral or negative. Whereas ambivalently insecure children do not quite know where they are in their relationships with attachment figures, the children in this category experience a predictable regime that lacks warmth, love and attention.

These children show little apparent signs of distress when they are separated from their parents. Upon reunion, the children either ignore or avoid their caregiver. Cuddles or comfort are not sought. These are watchful and wary children. Their play is perfunctory or desultory. They show little discrimination with whom they interact. Their's is a history of rejection and rebuff. They have learned that at times of distress or anxiety, attachment behaviour does not bring comfort and feelings of security. They have to develop ways of handling anxiety on their own. All trust in the adult world is lost. Other people are viewed as a source of potential hurt and pain. Emotionally speaking, it is therefore better to manage without them. The preferred strategy is to be emotionally independent, or even better, not to be an emotional being at all. Feelings are suppressed. If the desire for love and affection only seem to bring rejection, it may be better to try and live without them. So, whereas ambivalent children fear that they will not get what they want, avoidant children fear what they want. The self is not seen as lovable or likable. Self-esteem remains low.

Avoidant individuals find it difficult to make close relationships. Emotional involvement is avoided. There is the constant anxiety that intimacy will bring rejection and hurt. Avoidant personalities become 'compulsively self-reliant' (Bowlby 1973). In terms of the value and meaningfulness of both past and present relationships, these are 'dismissing' personalities (Main 1994, 1985; Howe 1995). However, the personality remains fragile. Conflict, anxiety and upset are not handled well and can often lead to emotional breakdown or violent outbursts or withdrawal.

Relationships with other people are shallow and indiscriminate. Little or no interest is taken in other people's feelings. People who show emotion or express needs are ignored or rejected, often in a hostile manner. For avoidant personalities, it is better to reject than be rejected. However, beneath the cold, unfeeling front, there is a great deal of uncertainty as well as insecurity. The emotional isolation brings loneliness and feelings of despair. Depression is never very far away.

Insecure, anxious and disorganised attachments

This category emerged as an attempt to understand the attachment behaviour of children who had been physically abused. The parent is not necessarily consistently rejecting, but he or she might occasionally be very hostile or scary. Displays of love and affection may occasionally be dispersed amongst the aggression and violence. Children experience their parents as either frightening (in the case of physical abuse) or possibly frightened (in the case of severe mental illness). In either case, the attachment figure's behaviour triggers the children's anxieties. Anxiety normally provokes attachment behaviour causing children to approach their caregiver. But the caregiver is a source of neither comfort nor safety, being the cause of the initial anxiety. The children are presented with an irresolvable conflict. Attachment behaviour pulls them towards their attachment figure whose behaviour frightens them away. The result is that children either literally or emotionally 'freeze'. The children are constantly confused in the presence of their caregivers. They show psychological disorganisation. By freezing and becoming emotionally absent, the children are trying to cope with the huge level of anxiety by some kind of psychological opt out. They attempt not to be present, so great is the dilemma.

Relationships with other people are a source of confusion. While the avoidant personality attempts emotional independence and denies need, and the ambivalent personality pesters people and clings on to relationships experiencing very mixed emotions, the disorganised personality is present but emotionally blank. There is little idea of what to do in relationships. They neither avoid them nor pursue them, but remain in a confused, somewhat helpless and distressed state. Early traumas remain 'unresolved' and this affects people's ability to deal with significant relationships both in the past and the present.

Nonattachments

These occur when children have not had an opportunity to develop any select-ive attachments whatsoever. The nature of their social environment has meant that it has not been possible to form affectional bonds with other people. This happens mainly when very young children are raised in residential institu-tions. They may be physically well looked after, but the constant changes of staff due to shift work and turnover mean that they are completely unable to develop selective attachments.

Such children are indiscriminate in their relationships; anyone it seems is as good as anyone else. People are interchangeable and matter so long as they hold out the prospect of meeting some current need. There is little distress experienced when people disappear out of their lives. Nonattached children have difficulty in controlling their impulses and feelings of anger and aggression. Deprived of continuous, consistent, reliable two-way intimacy, the personality is left poorly integrated. Other people represent opportunities for immediate gratification rather than the prospect of any long-term love and care, growth and development. Relationships are conducted at a superficial level. There is no reciprocity. So long as other people supply food, sex, shelter or activity, relationships with them are sustained. Feelings of frustration, impulsiveness, conflict and anger are easily roused, particularly if basic needs are not met or supplied. Marriages may be ended as quickly as they were started. And when people with little experience of selective attachments during their own childhood in turn become parents, they find it difficult to understand or meet the emotional needs of their children. Babies and toddlers can feel like competitors in the clamour for attention and gratification. The children's dependence can cause confusion and exasperation.

Nonattached children – who are still to be found in today's war zones, areas of famine, indeed any place where there is social upheaval – are likely to suffer the most profound developmental damage. This is why it is critical that social workers endeavour to place such children with families where they can form selective attachments and affectional bonds.

Attachment behaviours as adaptive responses

Depending on the nature and degree of emotional loss and anxiety experienced in the attachment relationship, children can adopt a number of defensive strategies. These strategies make perfect sense within the emotional climate of the attachment relationship. Thus, the behaviour of insecurely attached children must be seen as an adaptive response within the context of the relationship in which they find themselves. Each type of attachment behaviour is an attempt by the child to cope with the fears and anxieties generated by their relationship with their prime caregivers. 'Attachment behaviour is designed to bring proximity and security. When this goal is blocked or unforthcoming, the child has to develop psychological strategies that either attempt to ward off the anxiety or try to seek new ways of securing the attachment figure' (Howe 1995: 89). Each attachment pattern represents an attempt at psychological adaption and survival in a disturbed social relationship. They make sense within the context of the emotional environment in which the child finds himself or herself. They only become dysfunctional once the individual attempts to use his or her adaptive responses in relationships beyond that which he or she has with the caregiver. Insecure and anxious attachments are therefore functional insofar as they seek to protect the child against too much anxiety in situations where the caregiver is either unavailable, unreliable or hostile.

Children who experience inconsistency in parental warmth, responsive-

14

ness, love and care cope by trying to push their way back into the relationship by being demanding, seeking attention and not letting go and yet punishing the parent as the cause of the initial anxieties. This gives the child the feeling that he or she has some slight measure of control, but it feels fragile and unreliable. This is why the child feels in need and yet tries to resist being dependent on the attachment figure as provider – hence the *ambivalence*.

When caregivers are unloving, rejecting and hostile, unlike the resistant/ambivalent child, there is nothing he or she can do about it. The best adaptation is to try and become emotionally independent and self-contained – to be compulsively self-reliant. The child withdraws from relationships and *avoids* intimacy. Attempts to get close to people only seem to result in hurt. It is therefore prudent to go it alone.

Attachment theory and social work with children and their families

The three relationships which are most important during the life cycle are the ones most likely to reveal the individual's attachment history and personality type. They are (i) relationships with parents, (ii) relationships with a sexual partner, and (iii) relationships with one's own children (Bowlby 1988: 80). The quality and content of these relationships will depend on people's attachment histories, their innate temperamental make-up and the cultural context in which they find themselves. Child and family social workers work with all three types of relationship. An attachment perspective helps practitioners understand the character of particular relationships, indicates what the developmental consequences might be if a child remains in a particular relationship environment, and informs the making of placement decisions.

Aldgate (1991) provides a useful review of the relevance of attachment theory for child care social work. In broad terms, social workers have to consider how to maintain, strengthen or provide 'affectional bonds' and good quality attachment experiences for children brought to their attention. Behind these aims lies the concept of 'permanence'. Children need to secure permanent selective attachments to one or more loving and responsive caregivers if they are to achieve healthy psychological development. Aldgate (1991: 22) identifies three areas of practice which are informed by an attachment perspective:

1   A developmental approach endorses 'the importance of kinship attachments for children' and seeks 'to prevent long term family breakdown'. Within this outlook 'controlled separation' can be used, for example in the judicious use of respite care to enhance rather than sever kinship attachments.
2   When a child's attachment relationships have broken down or when they are damaging the child's emotional development, a permanent alternative

15

family will be needed 'who can repair the faulty attachment'. This may not rule out contact with the child's original family, but it is important that new warm, responsive relationships are established.

3   'Children can grow up in one family and retain links with another.'

We might add two more areas of practice which are supported by attachment theory and a developmental perspective:

4   Assessing the quality of relationships between parents and their partners, parents and their children, and children and their parents, and considering their impact on family life and children's development.
5   The provision of family support for parents and children experiencing stress.

The remaining chapters fill out these five rubrics. Throughout the following pages, we shall be meeting examples in which a developmental perspective informs research and practice in four key areas:

Assessments: Understanding the quality of relationships between parents, partners and children. (Chapter 2 by Marian Brandon, Chapter 3 by Gillian Schofield and Chapter 4 by Steven Parvez Rashid)
Outcomes: What happens when the quality of a child's care and attachment relationships are very poor and damaging. (Chapter 5 by Gwyneth Boswell)
Contact and Prevention: Practical attempts to maintain contact between children and absent or non-custodial parents. (Chapter 6 by Diana Hinings and Chapter 7 by Peter Wedge)
Placements and Support: Providing parents with support to help them look after their children and providing children with new substitute families. (Chapter 8 June Thoburn and Chapter 9 by Kate Pearson).

References

Ainsworth, M. D. S., Blehar, M.C., Waters, E. and Wall, S. (1978) *Patterns of Attachment*. New Jersey: Erlbaum.
Aldgate, Jane (1991) 'Attachment theory and its application to child care social work – an introduction.' In Joyce Lishman (ed.) *Handbook of Theory for Practice Teachers in Social Work*. London: Jessica Kingsley Publishers.
Bowlby, John (1961) *Attachment (Attachment and Loss I)* London: Hogarth Press.
Bowlby, John (1973) *Separation: Anxiety and Anger (Attachment and Loss II)*. London: Hogarth Press.

Bowlby, John (1979) *The Making and Breaking of Affectional Bonds* London: Tavistock.

Bowlby, John (1980) *Loss, Sadness and Depression (Attachment and Loss III).* London: Hogarth.

Bowlby, John (1984) 'The making and breaking of affectional bonds.' In BAAF (ed.) *Working with Children.* London: BAAF.

Bowlby, John (1988) *A Secure Base.* London: Routledge.

Frith, Uta (1989) *Autism: explaining the enigma.* Oxford: Blackwell.

Howe, David (1995) *Attachment Theory for Social Work Practice.* Basingstoke: Macmillan.

Howe, David and Hinings, Diana (1995) 'Reason and emotion in social work practice: managing relationships with difficult clients.' *Journal of Social Work Practice* 9:1 pp 5–14.

Main, Mary (1994) 'A move to the level of representation in the study of attachment organisation: implications for psychoanalysis'. Annual Research Lecture to the Psycho-Analytical Society: London, July 6.

Main, M. and Cassidy, J. (1988) 'Categories of response to reunion with the parent at age six' *Developmental Psychology* vol. 24, pp. 415–26.

Mattinson, Janet and Sinclair, Ian (1979) *Mate and Stalement.* London: Institute of Marital Studies.

Rutter, Michael (1991) 'A fresh look at maternal deprivation.' In Bateson, P. (ed.) (1991) *The Development and Integration of Behaviour.* Cambridge: Cambridge University Press.

Winnicott, D. W. (1965) *The Family and Individual Development.* London: Tavistock.

2 Attachment in child protection assessments: implications for helping

Marian Brandon

Assessment is familiar and comfortable territory for social workers. Making sense of, interpreting, and understanding problems is at the heart of social work practice. Assessment of the nature and quality of the parent/child relationship fits within this tradition. The significance of these ties between a parent and child are likely to be given consideration when moving a child from foster care to a permanent new home or back to birth parents. They appear to matter less, however, at the earlier stages in the child's contact with social services, when child protection is the central concern. Here the safety of the child is the main theme.

Safety is interpreted primarily as physical safety (danger to life and limb, and freedom from sexual assault) and rarely as emotional or psychological safety. Attachment and close relationships may be considered later, after a child protection conference has been held and patterns for dealing with the problems of maltreatment have often already been established. Alternatively the case may be filtered out of the system with no help at all because the risk to physical safety is low.

This chapter asks how an understanding of attachment and developing relationships fits into child protection work at the early stages; that is prior to a child protection conference, and in the more detailed assessment of harm or likely harm that might follow. The chronology of the child protection process will be examined with illustrations from case examples. I shall discuss whether knowing more about the nature of a child's attachment helps secure not only the child's safety, but also his or her welfare and general well being.

The context of child protection work

Changes in the ideologies and policies which have influenced assessment in child protection work, from the time of its re-emergence in the 1960s as 'the battered baby syndrome', have been extensively chronicled (see Parton 1991;

18

Frost and Stein 1987; and Cooper 1993). The impact of the child death enquiries is a common feature. Since the Colwell enquiry in 1973, there has been an increased emphasis on tight procedural detail, with the investigation of injury or abuse becoming a key theme. Risk assessment and monitoring of possible maltreatment has gradually taken the place of more supportive case-work skills and 'helping'.

The Beckford enquiry in the mid-1980's warned of the dangers to the safety of the child if social workers became overconcerned with the problems of the parents. Making allowances for parents' failings was interpreted as failing the child. The phrase 'the rule of optimism' dominated the criticism of parent-focused social work, and the expression 'child centred' began to gain currency. Assessment was to be scientific and predictive. Checklists of factors predisposing parents to abuse, or a child to be abused, were favoured, almost all of which included early mother/child bonding problems or attachment difficulties.

Numerous studies however, show the checklist approach, and particularly cycle of abuse theories, to be ineffective in predicting risk (for example Egeland in Gelles and Loeske 1991; Dingwall in Stevenson 1989). They argue that there is a need for *prospective* rather than *retrospective* studies to help us understand the likely chances of parents who have themselves been abused, abusing their own offspring. The numbers of inaccurate predictions (false positives) resulting from the checklist method, creates inefficiency in screening and targeting resources. By 1988, the 'Orange Book' Comprehens-ive Assessment guide reported that:

No simple checklist can be offered; indeed checklists are themselves potentially dangerous. (Department of Health 1988:12)

The guide does nevertheless provide several checklists itself which indic-ate significant features of parental background in relation to child abuse.

The Cleveland Inquiry (1988) shifted the emphasis yet again, and called into question 'child centred' practice which isolated the child from the context of the family. This practice was seen to be detrimental to the welfare of the child, and its criticism was encapsulated in the much quoted extract from the report: 'the child is a person and not an object of concern.'

The England and Wales Children Act 1989 came in response to these Inquiries, to lobbying groups like Family Rights Group and to research find-ings (particularly Social Work Decisions in Child Care 1985). Fox Harding (1991) points to the competing value positions in the Act, ranging from 'kinship defenders' to those who support 'psychological parents'. Both value positions are evident in the 'welfare checklist' in the Act, which attempts to balance the rightful place of the child within the birth family with the harm he or she could suffer from them.

Throughout the recent history of child abuse interventions, the regularity

19

with which relationship problems between parent and child occur in check-lists, and in profiles of abusing families, cannot be ignored. A recent review of risk assessment in the United States confirms this and indicates that the factors determining likely or continuing harm to the child that have the most empirical support are:

the child's age and developmental characteristics, the character of the abusive incident, actual levels of harm, the repetitive nature of the behaviour, the caregiver's impairment, and the personal history of abuse as a child, parent's recognition of the problem and ability to cooperate, parent's response to child behaviour, and parental level of stress and social support are also important. (English and Pecora 1994:463)

However, English and Pecora claim that although risk assessment is promoted as a decision making tool, risk models more often serve to verify or document decisions *already* made by workers. They conclude that:

caseworkers rely on intuitive processes based on supervision, experience, and training to make decisions. In the absence of empirical evidence, who is to say that these intuitive processes are better or worse than empirical models? (p 468)

Although the harm suffered by the child is the epicentre of child protection, the parents' capacity to behave as reasonable parents is an essential strand in the intervention in this field. It is in the assessment of parental capacity that the insights of attachment theory come into their own.

Attachment and child protection

Attachment is a powerful explanatory theory because it mixes the social with the psychological, and seeks to link what happens between a baby and her mother (or main caretaker) and the world that surrounds them. The consequences of these early relationships are played out throughout the child's life.

Impoverishment in early sense experience, impediments to the formation of human bonds, and conflicts between the baby and his human partners appear as recurrent themes in the developmental histories of many children and adults who suffer severe personality disorders. (Fraiberg 1980:3)

Attachment theory began as an attempt to understand the disturbed functioning of adults who had experienced traumatic losses or early separations, but became a theory of normal development that could offer explana-

20

tions for some types of a typical development. A means of categorising attachment relationships was developed by Ainsworth et al. (1978) in the laboratory technique known as the 'strange situation test'. This method has been adapted, but it remains a key model from which a parent–child relationship can be understood.

In the 'strange situation' a twelve to eighteen month old baby is left for a brief time in an unfamiliar room, confronted by a stranger, then reunited with the parent. This situation would normally be expected to create some anxiety in a baby of this age. The behaviour of the child on the parent's return provides a good indicator of the quality of the infant–parent relationship. The classifications developed from this test can also be used to describe the pattern of the relationship between older children and a parent. The parent's behaviour may also be indicative of their own attachment history. Four basic types of attachment behaviour are recognised (also see Chapter 1):

1 Secure attachment (Type B)

The behaviour of these infants is characterised by high levels of eye contact, vocalisation and a sense of mutuality in the relationship between the parent and her baby. The baby shows a preference for her parent over strangers and some distress at separation from the parent. The child seeks contact with the parent when reunited, is comforted quickly and then gets back to exploratory play.

Parental behaviour is on the whole responsive to the baby's needs, predictable and consistent. Over time, the growing child's repeated interaction with her parent leads her to form expectations that the parent is responsive and accessible. As a consequence, the child forms an idea of herself as competent and worthy of her parent's response. For these securely attached children, the occasional disappointment or anxiety will not be enough to upset the generally positive nature of the models of interaction.

2 Insecure/avoidant attachment (Type A)

Babies classified as insecure-avoidant show few signs of distress on separation. On return the baby avoids or ignores her parent and is watchful and wary. In general there is little discrimination in the baby's choice between her parent and strangers. The parent may be indifferent (neglectful) or insensitive to the baby, or alternatively try to provoke the baby into a response. Fonagy et al. describe how avoidant infants:

> appear disinterested, perhaps to forestall a further painful failure at communicating their emotional need to a detached caregiver or to reduce the anxiety engendered by an inappropriately intrusive one. (Fonagy et al. 1994:235)

21

3 Insecure/ambivalent attachment (Type C)

These children are highly distressed at separation and difficult to calm when reunited with the parent. The baby demands attention and angrily resists it simultaneously.

The care given to the child by the parent is generally inconsistent and insensitive to her needs. This pattern of response might be associated with parents who periodically neglect their child's needs.

4 Insecure/disorganised attachments (Type A/C or D)

These can be seen as a blend of types A and C, or alternatively they form a new type D. These infants show avoidant *and* ambivalent attachment behaviour. When reunited with the parent the baby is confused and disorganised in her behaviour. Many of these children freeze through reunion and separation, or make mechanical contact or gaze away. The parent is frightening or frightened and not a secure source of comfort to the child, thereby compounding the child's anxiety. The baby is faced with an irresolvable conflict since the source of comfort is also the source of confusion.

In two separate samples, Crittenden found that maltreated children who had experienced abuse, or abuse and neglect, were frequently classified in this group (Crittenden and Ainsworth 1989). These patterns were not only apparent in infants but also in pre-school age, maltreated children, for whom the Strange Situation would normally provoke little stress. Crittenden rejects the idea that this behaviour is disorganised. She claims the behaviour of these maltreated children is an attempt to resolve the conflict between the child's needs for proximity to the parent and her expectations that her parent will ignore, rebuff or punish her.

The bizarre and inconsistent behaviour of the D pattern has been singled out by many studies to be most characteristic of the severely deprived and maltreated child. Indeed Fonagy et al. (1994) claim that:

> Maltreatment appears fundamentally to jeopardise the organisation and development of the attachment relationship and the regulation of mental processes underlying social behaviour. (Fonagy et al. 1994:261)

Understanding the consequence of these behaviours as the child develops is important. The maltreated child needs proximity and contact just as much as do other children. Indeed Crittenden and Ainsworth (1989) explain that the child's experiences of previous maltreatment heighten distress during separation and make the need for contact more imperative. The value of using and adapting the Ainsworth classifications, for social workers, is in understanding the patterns of behaviour rather than seeking to replicate this test (see Howe 1995).

Anxious attachment through childhood

Like anxiously attached infants, older children (and adults) with anxious attachments tend be very preoccupied with the whereabouts of their attachment figure (Crittenden and Ainsworth 1989:443). Difficulty in separating from the attachment figure is combined with a lack of trust in him or her, to which is added chronic anger and resentment. Not surprisingly, there is commonly an inability to use support from the attachment figure when it is needed, or an apparent absence of feeling towards him or her. In these circumstances it is difficult for individuals to have the emotional sustenance provided by what Bowlby described as the 'secure base':

> human beings of all ages are found to be at their happiest and to be able to deploy their talents to best advantage when they are confident that, standing behind them, there are one or more trusted persons who will come to their aid should difficulties arise. The person trusted provides a secure base from which his (or her) companion can operate. And the more trustworthy the base the more it is taken for granted; and the more likely is its importance to be overlooked and forgotten. (Bowlby 1973:407)

Anxious attachment may stem from inappropriate responsiveness on the part of the parent. It may also have been prompted by a traumatic separation from, or permanent loss, of the attachment figure. Decisions taken in child protection work may have been responsible for these separations.

The social circumstances of neglected and maltreated children

The world of abused and neglected children is often one of multiple adversities and impoverishments. Gibbons' (1995) work identified 'vulnerability indicators' for children listed on the child protection register. In conferences where a child was considered to be vulnerable to abuse, a parent figure was found to have at least two of the following factors: substance abuse, a criminal record, psychiatric illness or violence to or from a partner. For many children whose names are added to the child protection register because they are suffering or likely to suffer significant harm, living with this adversity will also include experiencing a disturbed relationship with a mother or mother figure.

Rutter et al. list the types of adverse experience which indicate a high risk of psychiatric illness in childhood or adulthood (i.e. likely significant harm). They include changing and inconsistent caregiving, with mothers and fathers moving in and out of a child's life; family discord and quarrelling; and hostility and blame directed to the child (Rutter et al. 1990:151). These factors have similarities with Gibbons' list of vulnerability indicators and are reminiscent of Bowlby's (1988) description of mothers of difficult, unhappy or anxious children:

> mothers who are insensitive to their children's signals, perhaps because they are preoccupied and worried about other things, who ignore their children, or interfere with their children in an arbitrary way, or simply reject them. (Bowlby 1988:48)

Parental sensitivity, therefore, is a key factor in promoting a healthy attachment. It is defined by Ainsworth et al. (1978) as the ability to accurately perceive and interpret the infants' attachment signals, and to respond to them promptly and adequately. The success or failure of parental sensitivity will influence the kind of relationship which a parent and child will establish. In the psycho-social conditions described by Gibbons and Rutter, it is obviously much harder for parents to succeed.

Fahlberg demonstrates parental sensitivity to the child's signals very neatly in a diagram which she calls 'the positive cycle of interaction' (1994:29):

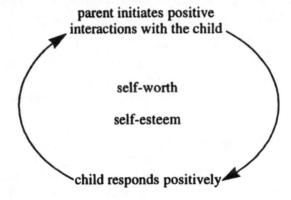

Fahlberg points out that as this cycle has only two parts it can be initiated by either adult or child.

It is possible for these positive interactions to come from important figures other than parents. Dunn's work demonstrates the significance of young children's close relationships with siblings and friends (Dunn 1993). Similarly, grandparents can be attachment figures for children.

Attachment and the Children Act 1989

There are several elements of the England and Wales Children Act which could put attachment into the assessment and intervention frame for social workers in child protection. A key theme in the Act is Family Support and the

24

notion of partnership with parents. Where children are separated from their families there is a presumption of continued contact. Intervention to encourage this contact and help heal damaged relationships will be an inevitable part of maintaining links. The extension of 'parental responsibility' through the child's life, even when a Care Order is made, puts the child squarely into the context of his or her family of origin.

The current debate about whether services are best targeted at children 'in need' (often characterised as preventive work) or children suffering or at risk of 'significant harm' (often characterised as child protection work) has been fuelled by the 1994 Audit Commission report *Seen But Not Heard*, and the Department of Health summaries of child protection research, *Messages from Research* (1995). Families where maltreatment or neglect is current or likely in the future, will probably fit both the 'need' and the 'harm' criteria for help and intervention. It could be argued that this group is the most in need of social work time and resources. Identifying these families will be a continuing priority, regardless of how they are fitted into the statutory framework.

The use of the term 'significant harm' as a determinant of the severity of maltreatment or neglect to a child has the potential to change the emphasis, away from looking for evidence of the actions of parents (for example bruises or other forensic evidence of maltreatment) and towards assessing the harm that is experienced by the child. By so doing, there is a requirement to look beyond single actions of parents to the totality of care that the child receives. This has the potential to broaden the understanding of harm, extending beyond mere physical safety to encompass freedom from significant emotional harm.

The significant harm section (31) of the Children Act, used when seeking a Care or Supervision Order, requires threshold conditions to be established before consideration can be given to making an Order. Significant harm encompasses ill treatment (physical, sexual, emotional or a combination of these) or harm to development (which might be physical, intellectual, emotional, social, or behavioural, or again any combination of these). It must be established that the harm is significant to that particular child, taking account of the child's own characteristics, including any factors which might promote resilience. The possibility of future, or likely significant harm also exists in the Act. This can include the harm continuing, or harm from particular circumstances manifesting themselves at a later stage.

In section 31 of the Act the significant harm must be attributable to deficits in care the child receives from the parent(s) (the reasonable parent test). Reasonable parenting is not an objective test, but must be matched to the needs of the particular child. The Guidance to the Act (Vol 1: para 3.11) makes clear that the local authority has a responsibility to offer help under Part 111 and Schedule 2 'which would be likely to improve the situation sufficiently' which might help parents become 'reasonable'.

A child with secure attachments could be said to have received a good

25

measure of reasonable parenting, although it may have come from sources other than the parent, for example grandparents or siblings. An insecure attachment, whilst not in itself indicating significant harm, nor necessarily likely significant harm, could be said to suggest some deficits in parenting. An alternative proposition would be that the characteristics of the particular child would make being a 'reasonable parent' much harder and that this child would be difficult for anyone to parent.

Thus the understanding of the harm a child receives depends upon an appreciation of their developing relationships. A secure attachment will be a good buffer against future harm or adversity and help to foster resilience (Fonagy et al. 1994), so an attached child could be said to be less likely to suffer harm in the future than a similar child without the same quality of relationships.

Yet the relationship between a child and her main caretakers is clearly not the only source of harm. The impact of harm from broader societal problems like poverty and discrimination, and inadequate road safety planning, or building design, should also be understood as part of a child's life experiences that contribute to significant harm.

The child protection process

What follows is a descriptive analysis of different children's routes through the child protection process. An examination is made of the way in which this process can take account of attachment relationships in the early stages of the assessment of significant harm. Three themes are pursued: firstly the need to get the early assessment right so that the most appropriate help is offered; secondly, how not to compound the harm through the use of the child protection process; and thirdly, possibilities for preventing significant harm by intervening where there are likely attachment problems.

Scott's entry into the child protection system was prompted by concerns arising from a routine hospital medical. Scott (aged three) was the first child of a violent partnership. Both parents are white and working class, and Scott's mother was said to have had a bleak, loveless childhood. His father made repeated suicide attempts in Scott's first year of life and lost his job. From birth, Scott needed special skin care and medical treatment because of severe eczema. He was placid and rarely made demands, in stark contrast to his father. Scott's mother said of her husband:

He demanded so much attention that Scott got left out. He used to flip out if he didn't. Scott just had to lay in his cot – I'll swear now that's why he's delayed.

Scott was well cared for physically as a young baby and his sore and sometimes raw skin never became infected. His global developmental delay was not properly recognised until his second year, when his mother started comparing his lack of progress with his new baby sister, who seemed a very different, much more responsive sort of baby. This baby was more able to express her needs and have them met by her mother, unlike Scott who was left alone in his cot.

By this time Scott's mother had formed a new partnership, and Scott's father had moved away, out of contact. This new relationship was with another controlling and exacting man. This was his first experience of parenting and he considered Scott to be a very unsatisfactory step-child. By the age of three Scott was walking very unsteadily, vocalising but not talking, and had what were described by professionals as 'a number of irritating habits'.

A routine hospital medical noticed Scott to be under-nourished, dehydrated, with several bruises (including around his buttocks) which were seen as indications of possible sexual abuse. These concerns brought Scott into the child protection system. The possibility of sexual abuse was discounted at an early stage in the investigation; the bruises were attributed to very rough handling, primarily, it was thought, by the step-father. Exasperated by Scott's inability to feed himself properly, and by his habit of banging his head on the floor, Scott's parents had attempted to 'train' him out of his bad habits.

The bruises and other signs of possible maltreatment were an indication of a host of problems, one of which was Scott's parents' reluctance to acknowledge his disabilities. There was no longer any positive cycle of interaction between Scott and his parents. Any positive interactions that might have existed were undermined by the punitive training and discouragement that characterised Scott's recent experiences at home. Meal times and toileting were horrific events for Scott and his family.

The cycle of interaction between Scott and his parents at this stage is depicted as follows:

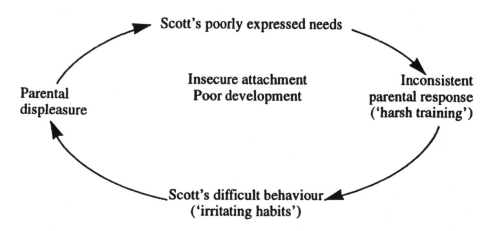

Scott's poorly expressed needs

Insecure attachment
Poor development

Parental displeasure

Inconsistent parental response ('harsh training')

Scott's difficult behaviour ('irritating habits')

Scott had always been a difficult baby and child, which increased his risk of maltreatment (Scott's circumstances are very similar to English and Pecora's (1994) clutch of factors listed earlier). Scott was also compared unfavourably by his parents to his sister. Dunn (1993) points out the implications of not matching up to a sibling, claiming that what matters developmentally:

> is not only how loved or attended to by the mother or father a child feels, but also how loved or attended to he feels compared with his siblings (Dunn, 1993:85–86).

Because of his disabilities Scott was, by definition, a child 'in need' (s17(c)), and thus eligible for services, without requiring access to services via the child protection system. At the time of the child protection referral however, the services provided were not preventing Scott from suffering significant harm. At this early time of assessment, Scott was being harmed by a lack of parental sensitivity to his needs. The harm he was suffering was in a number of areas encompassing physical, emotional and social development as well as the ill-treatment which was evident in the bruising. It is doubtful, however, whether Scott's plight would have become a child protection concern if there had not been bruising and fears of sexual abuse.

One of the problems in safeguarding Scott's wellbeing was in acknowledging that he *was* suffering significant harm. The fact that he was a disabled child made this harder for professionals to recognise. It was difficult to disentangle the harm stemming from his disability from the harm stemming from a lack of parental sensitivity, and indeed as Scott's mother hinted in the earlier quote, the two may have been connected. (Scott and his parents were subsequently offered intensive help and support which included a brief period of foster care for Scott. The relationship between Scott and his parents is gradually improving.)

Separation as protection

The nature of the relationship between parent and child should be borne in mind when determining whether or not to separate a child from her carer. (This was important in planning Scott's separation from his mother.) The harm to the child from the maltreatment should be balanced with the likely harm stemming from the separation and the insecurity it might promote. This would include 'enforced accommodation' that might be used in place of an Emergency Protection Order (EPO) to keep a child safe.

This was an issue for Abigail (aged nine) and her two brothers (aged five and two). These children were 'accommodated' in foster care for three nights with their mother's reluctant, and ill informed, consent to avoid an EPO, while enquiries into allegations of sexual abuse by a family acquaintance were made. There were fears that the mother may also have been involved in the abuse. The mother was denied contact with her children.

The mother, a single parent, had mild learning disabilities and a history of allowing men with offences against children into the household. She also suffered from ill health and from time to time was unable to cope with her children. Her behaviour oscillated between being very responsive to the children's needs, and being emotionally unavailable. Abigail's behaviour at school had always been difficult and attention seeking, and recently had become worse. Her unpredictable relationship with her mother had created some insecurities in her attachment, but she was able to use her mother as a support figure.

The serious abuse of Abigail was substantiated (and a year later the abuser was convicted and received a long prison sentence). The mother was not in any way implicated in the sexual abuse and there was no evidence of abuse to the two younger children. Abigail's immediate safety had not been under threat because the alleged abuser was in custody. The harm to Abigail from the sexual abuse was compounded by separation from her mother, her strongest support figure. The other two children, who had not previously suffered significant harm, had been denied contact with their mother for no good reason, and were thus at risk of suffering 'system abuse' by being 'protected'. Precipitate, ill thought-out action compounded problems in a family already struggling to cope, and where attachments were insecure.

The child protection conference and beyond

At each stage of the child protection process cases are screened out. Gibbons' study of 1,888 cases found that 26% of these were filtered out by the time of the investigative interview and a further 50% were filtered out following this interview. This left 24% of cases to be considered by the child protection conference and only 15% of the original number were registered (Gibbons 1995). Thus a child protection conference will take place in a minority of cases under investigation. For those cases filtered out of the system it is unlikely that help will have been offered, although it may have been needed.

The child protection conference has limited powers (whether or not to place the child's name on the register, to allocate a key worker, to create a child protection plan) but considerable influence. It will establish the pattern of help which is to follow, if indeed help is to be offered.

Paul, aged seven, came into the child protection system and was the subject of an initial child protection conference because of reports by his mother to Social Services of sexualized and generally difficult behaviour by Paul. The sexualized behaviour had occurred since Paul and a friend found a pornographic magazine in the woods and re-enacted its contents. Paul's difficult behaviour for the last three or four months had included verbal and physical abuse to his mother and threats of suicide. Paul's mother had considered asking the education department to provide boarding education for him because she had trouble coping. Paul's mother is a single parent, living on state benefit. Paul has no contact with his father and irregular, but, to him, significant contact with his step-father. Paul's mother has a history of sexual abuse and depression.

At the child protection conference the plan was to register Paul under the category of sexual abuse, to make a referral for assessment at a family psychiatric centre, and to provide Paul with 'keep safe' work. The conference chairperson would not allow the conference to discuss issues beyond the incident that triggered the conference. The social worker, who knew the family well, was aware of long-standing relationship problems between mother and son, hinted at by the problems in his behaviour. Thus, both the plan and the understanding of the problems were skewed by a recent incident, and attempts were made to gather more information about likely harm from sexual abuse, rather than an appreciation of the whole context of Paul's care and needs.

An understanding of the nature of Paul's attachment to his mother was essential to making sense of the difficulties they were experiencing together and apart. Three months after the child protection conference, Paul was accommodated because things at home were no better and his mother could no longer cope. He was restless and unhappy when he was seeing his mother only monthly. When the contact was increased to once a fortnight he was much less anxious, and settled well, making good progress in school. Paul's ambivalent attachment made it harder for him to sustain lengthy periods without contact with his mother.

Understanding attachment to prevent significant harm

Current research emphasises that insecure attachment cannot be considered pathological in itself. Interventions which attempt to break the cycle of insecure attachment are valid, particularly where they attempt to change parents' understanding of their own relationship problems with their parents and carers, what has been called: 'their perception of their attachment biography' (Van IJzendoorn et al. 1995:226).

Typical of families needing intervention in this way are those described so graphically by Fraiberg:

> In each of these cases, the baby has become a silent partner in a family tragedy. The baby in these families is burdened by the oppressive past of his parents from the moment he enters the world. The parent, it seems, is condemned to repeat the tragedy of his childhood with his own baby in terrible and exacting detail. (Fraiberg, 1980:165)

The system of pre-birth child protection conferences allows for babies carried by mothers with worrying biographies and other difficulties to be offered protection from likely significant harm. Assessment of the potential of the parent or parents to be good enough attachment figures, and support to help before problems become established are made *possible* by this system. A description follows of contrasting intervention and planning set in motion by child protection conferences for two pregnant young women. Both unborn babies were registered in the category of 'likely neglect'.

Sarah was a sixteen year old living in residential care. She was no longer in contact with the baby's father and little was known about this relationship. Her career in care started when she was four, when her mother said she could not cope with Sarah and her two siblings. Sarah experienced two foster and two adoptive placement breakdowns. Since living in children's homes she had a pattern of absconding. She received two convictions for arson when she was fourteen and fifteen, and because it was felt Sarah posed an unacceptable fire hazard, no mother and baby units would take her. Sarah's care of herself varied from good to total disregard. The pyschiatrist's report said:

Sarah has never experienced consistent nurturing and she is only able to make superficial relationships. Her level of maturity is such that she could not care for a baby.

In the child protection plan, arrangements were made for support for Sarah up to, during, and after the birth, by both residential workers and her social worker. The baby, Jordan, was removed from his mother the day after his birth and has subsequently been placed for adoption. Support for Sarah dwindled after Jordan's birth.

The pattern of Sarah's life, the separation from her mother and subsequently her siblings, the repeated breakdown of placements and relationships and the fire raising, were used as evidence of Sarah's likely inability to care adequately for her baby. The baby's right not to risk a damaged relationship with his mother superseded Sarah's right to try to be a parent. An assessment of Sarah's own attachment deficits was thus used as an argument to remove Jordan. It was not used as an argument for Sarah having continued support either to keep her baby and to be a reasonable parent, nor to come to terms with relinquishing him.

Tamsin was a nineteen year old who had left care, pregnant, eighteen months previously. This was to be her second child. Her first baby had been compulsorily removed because of neglect and under stimulation. Tamsin was said to be still unable to meet her own needs and had a history of harming herself. From the age of ten Tamsin was in care and rehabilitation home was never possible. Most of her adolescence had been in residential care.

Tamsin's relationship with the unborn baby's father (a married man who denied paternity) ended violently. Tamsin had recently fallen out with her family who refused to help her. She claimed 'I'm nineteen now and don't need my parents.'

The GP commented:

Tamsin, who has lurched from crisis to crisis throughout her life, will continue to do so, and will need help.

Tamsin, however, resisted help. The professionals at the child protection conference (which Tamsin also attended) were despairing of Tamsin, saying history was repeating itself and Tamsin was impossible to help. The bare minimum of checks and monitoring by the ante-natal services were to be attempted, and the local authority was to consult with the legal department to debate possible legal options before the next conference.

Within weeks of the conference Tamsin married a new boyfriend and moved with him to another part of the country. Tamsin's baby, Claire, was born five weeks premature by emergency caesarean section weighing three pounds. She was in an incubator in special care for four weeks. Tamsin blamed the baby for the pain she suffered after the birth. Tamsin did not bond with the baby and needed encouragement to feed and hold her.

The support plan offered by the new area involved a residential unit for Tamsin and her baby. Staff were positive about the developing relationship between mother and baby in spite of poor beginnings. Tamsin felt trusted as a parent and responded to the care and attention given her. She in turn was able to offer good care to her baby, although with the baby in her sole care, Tamsin was stressed and had difficulty coping. Tamsin had unrealistic expectations of the baby and attributed inappropriate intention to her behaviour.

The Family Centre Assessment at twelve weeks commented that Claire had started to attach to Tamsin. Tamsin had also begun to respond more readily towards her baby and there were signs of an ability to meet the baby's physical and emotional needs.

The health visitor was in regular contact when Tamsin returned home and was delighted with Claire's progress in her parents' care. Tamsin responded well with both her health visitor and her social worker saying:

They had faith in me, they knew I could do it.

Within weeks however Tamsin and her husband moved again to another area. Tamsin did not like her new social worker and was in regular violent conflict with her husband. When the couple separated, leaving Tamsin to look after Claire alone, the baby's care deteriorated.

At seven months Claire was removed on an Emergency Protection Order and placed with foster carers.

Tamsin's response to the help offered her was that of an insecurely attached adult. She was angry and demanded help and attention whilst at the same time rejecting it. Yet the early help given to Claire had been very fruitful and Tamsin had begun to trust and rely on others. However, Tamsin ran from this help and could not recreate these positive relationships later. Tamsin was not able to be a reasonable parent for Claire, whose attachments are consequently likely to be impaired.

There is room for some slight optimism for Tamsin as a parent. In the right circumstances with workers who could understand and withstand her rejections, she could perhaps be helped to understand her own attachment biography. This may be too late for her as a parent to Claire.

Conclusions

There are strong arguments for a better understanding of developing relationships at the early stages in child protection work. Taking attachments into account helps to ensure that early plans and decisions are made that safeguard the child *and* promote his or her welfare. These very early assessments are important because they dictate not only the pattern of work which is to follow, but also whether or not help will be offered.

Once the harm and the sources of harm are made more clear the pattern of helping becomes more apparent. Critics (e.g. Lynch 1993) have argued that the child protection system is still geared to the investigation of incidents, not the process of harm itself. Neglect and emotional abuse may not come into the system because there is no single identifiable incident. For Scott, it was not until an *incident* causing bruising occurred that the overall harm, including damaged developing relationships, was considered. This was even more the case with 'Paul'. Paul's early assessment did not take account of harm to him from a range of sources including his relationship with his mother. For this reason plans to protect him did not promote his welfare adequately.

For Paul and Claire a detailed examination of their pattern of attachment could also have helped to prepare them for moves and plan contact with family members. For Paul the unexplored area of attachment to his stepfather might have provided him with a less regular, but satisfying contact that was not characterised by ambivalence, unlike his relationship with his mother. In Scott's case, understanding the connections between his relationships, his developmental delay and his maltreatment provided a clearer focus for social work with the child and the family.

Parents' own attachment deficits can be acknowledged, creating the possibility of planning work to help to banish what Fraiberg described as the 'ghosts in the nursery'. This would encourage parents' sensitivity to their child's needs. (This work was tried to an extent with Tamsin and not embarked on at all with Sarah.) Use can also be made of specific nurturing resources. An example of this would be to enlist voluntary organisations like

33

'Newpin', which have volunteer workers who nurture parents who have maltreated or neglected their children.

It is important to bear in mind the 'sleeper' effect of attachment work with parents mentioned by Van IJzendoorn (1995). No immediate improvement in sensitivity between parent and child is sometimes seen but changes in the parent's representations of their own attachment might have positive effects later.

If parents only acquire new behavioral strategies to interact with their infant, they may not be able to find ways to deal with the attachment needs of the developing child . . . It may take more time to change mental representations than to learn new behavioral strategies . . . (Van IJzendoorn, 1995:245)

The damage caused by child protection investigations is acknowledged by many sources (Audit Commission 1994, Thoburn et al. 1995, Cleaver and Freeman 1995). Positive plans to help the child and family could compensate for the often fruitless intrusion of an investigation.

References

Adcock, M., Hollows, A. and White, R. (1994) *Child Protection Update.* London: National Children's Bureau.

Ainsworth, M., Bleher, M., Water, E., and Wall, S. (1978) *Patterns of Attachment: A Psychological Study of the Strange Situation.* New Jersey: Erlbaum.

Audit Commission. (1994) *Seen but not Heard: Co-ordinating Community Child Health and Social Services for Children in Need.* London: HMSO.

Cleaver, H. and Freeman, P. (1995) *Parental Perspectives in Cases of Suspected Child Abuse.* London: HMSO.

Cooper, D. (1994) *Child Abuse Revisited: Children, Society and Social Work.* Buckingham: Oxford University Press.

Crittenden, P. and Ainsworth, M. (1989) 'Child maltreatment and attachment theory' in eds Cicchetti, D. and Carlson, V. *Child Maltreatment.* Cambridge: Cambridge University Press.

Department of Health. (1988) *Protecting Children: A Guide for Social Workers Undertaking a Comprehensive Assessment.* London: HMSO.

Department of Health. (1991) *Working Together under the Children Act 1989: A guide to arrangements for interagency co-operation for the prevention of children from abuse.* London: HMSO.

Department of Health. (1995) *Studies in Child Protection: Messages from Research.* London: HMSO.

DHSS. (1985) *Social Work Decisions in Child Care: Recent Research Find-*

ings and their Implications. London: HMSO.

Dingwall, R., Eekelaar, J. and Murray, T. (1983) *The Protection of Children: State Intervention and Family Life*. Oxford: Basil Blackwell.

Dunn, J. (1993) *Young Children's Close Relationships: Beyond Attachment*. Newbury Park, California: Sage.

English D. and Pecora P. (1994) 'Risk assessment as a practice method in child protective services', *Child Welfare League of America* LXXIII (5): 451–473.

Fahlberg, V. (1994) *A Child's Journey Through Placement*. London: BAAF.

Fonagy P., Steele M., Steele H., Higgit, A. and Target, M. (1994) 'The Emmanuel Miller Memorial Lecture 1992 – The Theory and Practice of Resilience', *Journal of Child Psychology and Psychiatry*, 35 (2): 231–257.

Fox-Harding, L. (1992) *Perspectives in Child Welfare*. London: Longmans.

Fraiberg, S., ed. (1980) *Clinical Studies in Infant Mental Health: The First Year of Life*. London: Tavistock Publications.

Frost, R. and Stein, M. (1987) *The Politics of Child Welfare*. Hemel Hempstead: Harvester Wheatsheaf.

Gelles, R. and Loseke, D., eds. (1993) *Current Controversies on Family Violence*. Newbury Park, California: Sage.

Gibbons, J., Conroy, S. and Bell, C. (1995) *Operating the Child Protection System*. London: HMSO.

Howe, D. (1995) *Attachment Theory for Social Work Practice*. Basingstoke: Macmillan.

Lynch, M. (1992) 'Child protection – Have we lost our way?', *Adoption and Fostering*, 16 (4): 15–22.

Parton, N. (1991) *Governing the Family: Child Care, Child Protection and the State*. Basingstoke: Macmillan.

Rutter, M., Quinton, D. and Hill, J. (1990) 'Adult outcomes of institution-reared children: males and females compared' cited in Howe, D. (1995) *Attachment Theory for Social Work Practice* Basingstoke: Macmillan.

Van IJzendoorn, M., Juffer, F. and Duyvesteyn. M. (1995) 'Breaking the inter-generational cycle of insecure attachment: A review of the effects of attachment-based interventions on maternal sensitivity and infant security', *Journal of Child Psychology and Psychiatry* 36 (2): 225–248.

Stevenson, O., ed. (1989) *Child Abuse: Public Policy and Professional Practice* Hemel Hempstead: Harvester Wheatsheaf.

Thoburn. J., Lewis, A. and Shemmings, D. (1995) *Paternalism or Partnership? Family Involvement in the Child Protection Process*. London: HMSO.

3 Attachment theory, neglect and the concept of parenting skills training: the needs of parents with learning disabilities and their children

Gillian Schofield

There has recently been increasing concern among those involved in child care social work and those involved in the court system about long running cases involving allegations of neglect in families where parents, and in particular mothers, have learning disabilities. At the outset I need to stress that these extreme problems affect a minority of parents with a learning disability – my concern in this chapter is about those parents who have serious difficulties in meeting the emotional, educational and physical needs of their children and whose children come to the attention of social workers, health visitors, General Practitioners, teachers and so on. Equally the difficulties which these parents experience are not unique to parents with learning disabilities. What I am trying to explore is whether when these two occur together, the learning disability and the parenting problems, the models for understanding what has gone wrong and therefore the kind of help that is offered make sense. Specifically I am interested in whether a focus on attachment may assist in understanding and ameliorating the relationship between mother and child and ultimately lessen the need for children to be separated from their parents.

In reviewing my own recent work as a Guardian *ad Litem*, I discovered that a significant number of recent cases involved a mother with some degree of learning disability. The learning disability was never the only factor, indeed mothers had often experienced a pattern of separation, loss and abuse in childhood, which had continued into adult life. The professionals involved, however, felt that the learning difficulty was the key to the parenting problems and would cause special concern. In these cases there had often been a great deal of effort and resources put into multi-agency packages of support and parenting skills training. However there seemed to be certain problems in the interaction between parents and children which were very resistant to change. There was a consensus among the professional network that there was an affectionate relationship between child and parent, sometimes referred to as an attachment, and yet during the pre-school years the children became increasingly out of control and experienced low self-esteem and developmental delays, especially in language development. There was often a strong feeling that the parents should not be blamed because the problems were not their 'fault' but in time both parents and professionals were forced to acknowledge that the children's needs, particularly emotional and intellectual, were not being met. For me it has sometimes felt as if all the intensive work, the packages of 'support', were in some sense missing the point. This chapter sets out to clarify what I mean by that.

The questions which arise from some of these histories relate to the connections between the nature of the parenting behaviour, the quality of the attachments and the likelihood of physical and emotional neglect – and whether the support and parenting skills training which is offered is meeting the needs of the families who cause most concern. In terms of cases which reach child protection procedures and ultimately courts, the issue in relation to attachment is whether an impoverished relationship can itself lead to significant harm in terms of the impairment of social, emotional, intellectual and behavioural development. If so, what are the observable behaviours in parent and child which give evidence of this process at work? Is parenting what you do, what you think or what you feel? From the point of view of children of parents with learning disabilities, there is an additional question – do cognitive deficits which might be thought to cause difficulties in mastering practical tasks also contribute to problems in establishing secure attachments or do other aspects of personal circumstances and history combine with the cognitive deficit to cause difficulties in parenting? Or is the learning disability irrelevant to the causation of the problems but perhaps important to how help should be offered?

These are controversial questions to ask but for those of us who are involved in thinking through what can be helpful to parents and children and in some cases making decisions as to whether a child can be looked after in her own family, there is a pressing need to make sense of what is going on between the parent and the child and to put it in a theoretical framework. The aim here is therefore to pull together some ideas on attachment, some ideas on neglect and some ideas on the parenting capacity of parents with learning disabilities in order to make connections between parenting behaviour, family relationships and the risk of harm to children's development. A further connection needs to be made, tentatively at this stage, with the nature of the services which are offered to families and the extent to which the learning disability is taken into account. These connections will then be explored through reference to case material to test their usefulness.

In this chapter , I shall for convenience refer to 'mother' as the most likely primary attachment figure. This is not to suggest that fathers and other members of extended families cannot be attachment figures for children. On the contrary, we know that children form multiple attachments from babyhood onwards and any model for understanding the emotional development of children would need to be aware of the benefits to children of the availability of other committed carers.

Attachment and parenting behaviour

This section will move towards establishing the theoretical framework for understanding the impact of parenting behaviour on the nature of attachment. The way in which the baby moves through phases towards establishing a secure attachment has been well documented by Bowlby and others (Bowlby 1969). The parent's behaviour has received rather less attention although Bowlby makes clear that the quality of the attachment will depend on the sensitivity of the mother. The idea of the mother-child interaction as a cycle of action and reaction is central. As Bowlby puts it:

> Throughout these cycles the baby is likely to be as spontaneously active as his mother. Where their roles differ is in the timing of their responses. Whereas an infant's initiation and withdrawal from interaction tend to follow his own autonomous rhythm, a sensitive mother regulates her behaviour so that it meshes with his. In addition she modifies the form her behaviour takes to suit him: her voice is gentle but higher pitched than usual, her movements slowed, and each next action adjusted in form and timing according to how her baby is performing. Thus she lets him call the tune and by a skilful interweaving of her own responses with his creates a dialogue. (Bowlby 1988:7)

These cycles operate in the feeding situation from the earliest days, when babies pause at intervals as if programmed to set up the interaction. The dialogue of feeding and pausing, crying and cuddling, smiling and eye contact is central to establishing the attachment. Out of the repetition of these cycles over time comes the child's sense of her mother as a secure base, as someone who can be relied on to be available physically and emotionally and who can be returned to after exploration of the wider world. The child gradually begins to build a working model not only of the ways in which the physical world behaves, in that if she drops a toy it breaks, but also a model of how parents and significant others behave and how, most importantly, she is expected to behave. The *reciprocity* and the *co-operation* set up from the earliest exchanges between child and parent are said by Bowlby to lay the foundation for what will come later. The existence of the secure base facilitates all other areas of development. Without it, the child is using its energy to ensure proximity to the attachment figure rather than being free to explore her environment and learn.

These early processes which establish themselves during the first year of life are well known. They overlap to a considerable extent with aspects of object relations theory in which the sensitivity of the 'good enough' mother is described in terms of primary maternal preoccupation and the mother's ability to 'keep the child in mind' while containing infantile anxiety (Winnicott 1965). These ideas help elucidate aspects of attachment formation and will be helpful in thinking in detail about difficulties in very early relationships.

Bowlby also went on to develop a framework for thinking about the ways in which the parent/child relationship develops during the next phase of the child's life. Since the pre-school period is a time when many relationship problems arise, particularly in relation to the establishment of control, it seems useful to look at this in more detail. Bowlby describes the reciprocity of these early years as a process of enlisting the child's co-operation. This is a particularly helpful idea. We know that once the relationship between a pre-school child and a parent has become à battle ground it is very hard to implement parenting which can establish a truce in which the child is inclined to find co-operation rewarding. It's hard to take the child/parent relationship back to the beginning and reverse destructive patterns of interaction.

In a further elaboration of this aspect of attachment, Bowlby describes a period of transformation between the ages of three and five during which the child develops the 'capacity to conceive of his mother as having her own goals and interests separate from his own and to take them into account' (Bowlby 1982). The significance of this process is that potentially it leads to collaboration between the child and the mother as part of a process of 'conceptual perspective taking'. This stage is not automatic and has to build on the earlier cycles. It seems that the ability of the child to develop this capacity is linked to the child's earlier experiences. Bowlby refers to research by Light (1979) which found that 'a mother who usually takes account of her child's perspective and interests is likely to have a child who reciprocates by taking account of his mother's perspective and interests.' In Light's research, mothers who scored highly in perspective taking were as much concerned with a child's feelings and intentions as with his actual behaviour and were prepared to make reasonable concessions when the situation warranted it, whereas mothers of low scorers took a more authoritarian line. For example, in answer to the question, 'What happens if you ask your child to do something for you and he says he can't because he's busy, in the middle of a game or something?', the high scoring mother would say, 'If he's doing something, I'll say do it when you're finished and he will.' A low scoring mother would be more likely to say, 'You'll do it now – I've told you to do it.' Thus making concessions and negotiating is contrasted with resorting to a more rigid and potentially more negative approach. Most parents will use a range of parenting strategies but here Bowlby is highlighting an important dimension.

Given Bowlby's emphasis on the importance of conceptual perspective taking in child development, it is useful to think about the overlap between what might be seen as loving a child, an emotional process, and the cognitive process of being able to take a child's perspective. The value of the cognitive process is that in time the child can take the parent's perspective and eventually build perspective taking, or perhaps what we might think of as empathy, into the way she relates to people in general. Although this process is not widely acknowledged in the literature on abuse and neglect, Crittenden and Ainsworth (1989) include the issue in their analysis of the links between attachment theory and child maltreatment.

> Should the parent herself (or himself) be handicapped either in perspective taking or in being able to communicate motivation, feelings, and plans to the child, the child's latent capacities for perspective taking and for clearer communication may well remain undeveloped or if developed, be likely to fail in producing mutual understanding and trust. (Crittenden and Ainsworth 1989:436)

Vera Fahlberg, a child psychotherapist who has been very influential in the application of attachment theory to social work practice, also uses the notion of cycles to describe the attachment process (Fahlberg 1988). She takes as the starting point the child expressing a need and being in a state of high arousal until that need is met. Once the parent meets the need the child is quiescent and relaxed until the next need arises and so the cycle goes round, many times in the course of a day. Out of this cycle, according to Fahlberg, comes a sense of security and attachment (Figure 3.1).

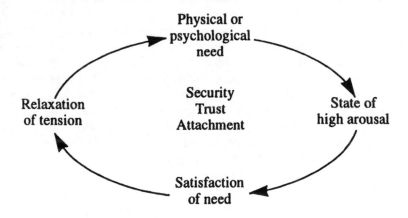

Figure 3.1 The arousal–relaxation cycle

The quality of the relationship, Fahlberg argues, is the means to an end, that end being the healthy development of the child. Attachment, she suggests, helps the child:

- attain full intellectual potential
- sort out what he or she perceives
- think logically
- develop social emotions
- develop a conscience
- trust others
- become self-reliant
- cope better with stress and frustration
- reduce feelings of jealousy
- overcome common fears and worries
- increase self-worth. (Fahlberg 1991: 14)

Some of these elements connect straightforwardly with the idea that the development of one strong relationship can lead to healthier future relationships and increased confidence. The other two strands are less obvious – these involve aspects of cognitive and moral development. Although the fact that children who experience poor care often have problems in learning, the connections between relationship or emotional difficulties and cognitive development are rarely made explicit and are often put down in a rather vague way to lack of stimulation. However there seems to be a more fundamental connection. For example, if we take Fahlberg's own model, the way in which the child learns about predictability in parental responses enables her to learn about cause and effect and this is the beginning of making sense of the world. Predictability in relationships also enables a child to begin to allow symbols to represent people, the transitional object, or to anticipate an event, the noise of food being prepared in the kitchen. Giving meaning to symbols and understanding causal relationships are significant parts of learning about the workings of the environment and have obvious connections with language development and other forms of learning. As Gesell (1940) has pointed out, these early experiences are part of 'learning to learn'. Fahlberg (1991) describes how the child's increasing ability to make sense of what she perceives is a key to this process.

If we look again at the list of benefits which Fahlberg has produced, it embraces key elements in the emotional, intellectual, social, moral and behavioural development of the child. With the exception of moral development, it is the impairment of these areas of development which is part of the Children Act definition of ' significant harm' (Children Act 1989 S31.9). It is the *level* of impairment which preoccupies social workers and courts in terms of decisions about intervention in family life. If we are to accept the links which Fahlberg makes between attachment and these other areas of development then an analysis of the attachment relationships in families where there are developmental concerns about the children would be central. Indeed the use of Fahlberg's charts in the Department of Health guidance, *Protecting Children – A Guide to a Comprehensive Assessment* (1989) suggests that even

41

though the theoretical basis may not be familiar to all social workers, these links are acknowledged at the assessment stage.

Although Fahlberg's model is very similar to Bowlby's, the use of the concept of arousal and relaxation is helpful not only in understanding the process by which attachments come about but also in giving a framework for explaining what can happen when the mother is not able to establish the rhythms described by Bowlby. For assessment purposes, we need as much detail as possible of what is going on when the cycles are not going round. Fahlberg suggests that the child whose needs are not met is left in a state of high arousal such that she experiences distress. If the cycles get repeatedly stuck at this point, this may lead in time to the child getting out of touch with their own needs and no longer expressing them. The child does not learn the connection between being hungry and being fed, perhaps receiving too much food when not hungry and not having her hungriness responded to at other times. Getting out of touch with bodily sensations is very apparent among children who seem not to feel the cold in winter and in summer wear too many clothes.

The cycles then can be interrupted at different points. Thinking through the connections with Light's 'perspective taking', it could be seen that the mother who negotiates with the child over whether the child will finish a game before doing a job is simply acknowledging that the child has needs, such as the need to play, and feelings, such as excitement or frustration, which must be taken into account. The child and mother have competing needs and feelings. Both will compromise, the mother waiting and the child doing the job before returning to the game.

In addition to the needs led arousal–relaxation cycle, Fahlberg proposes the existence of a positive parent – child interactional cycle (Figure 3.2).

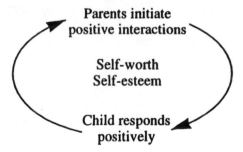

Figure 3.2 The cycle of positive interactions

It is important that the parent as well as the child will be positively initiating pleasurable social interactions, which are at least as important as the routine care of the child. Because this is said to contribute to the development of self-esteem, it is a fundamental unifying concept. The child may be quite happy playing but the mother checks gently to see if the child is cold and needs a cardigan. The child gets the message that even when she is not thinking of her mother and not communicating a need, her mother has kept her 'in mind' and is concerned for her welfare. Also the child learns that the parent keeps her in mind even when the child is playing quietly. It doesn't take naughty behaviour to remind the parent of the child's existence.

So if the idea of the attachment cycles and the role which the parent has to play in being sensitive to the child's own rhythms and in building the child's self-esteem is central to areas of child development, we need to know more about why some parents respond to their children in a way which encourages attachment and others do not. Specifically for the purposes of understanding the parenting capacity of parents with learning disabilities, we obviously need to know more about whether there is any information about the impact of cognitive deficits on those parenting behaviours which facilitate the development of secure attachments. This is a minefield in the research literature. However for social workers and other professionals who have to make decisions about interventions in the lives of families, it is not enough to conclude this section with a demand for more research. We have to try to work with what we know now.

Attachment problems and the concept of neglect

If there are concerns about the welfare of individual children, then we need to know if the problems they are experiencing are amenable to intervention and if so what kind of interventions might be helpful with which problems. This requires some attempt at establishing causal relationships between behaviours on the one hand and relationships on the other. If we have no models of causation it is difficult to see how areas of necessary change could be identified.

We have some ideas about what kinds of parental behaviour lead to secure attachments. In considering what constitutes behaviour which leads to various degrees of insecure attachment, we could simply say that it is the absence of these attachment producing behaviours. This of course is entirely compatible with some dictionary definitions of neglect of a certain task, 'to leave undone, omit to do'. However also part of the definition of neglect is the idea of 'to slight, disregard, not pay attention to'. Thus we have the notion of the parent omitting to do certain acts for the child but also the idea of the parent disregarding or perhaps ignoring the child. Although certain events might come into both categories, for example, not changing a baby's nappy, there is a difference between not thinking that frequent nappy changing is necessary and disregarding the child's feelings. We need to go back to the idea which features strongly in attachment theory although it has its roots in object relations theory, the parent needs to *keep the child in mind*. If we are using the concept of attachment to think about neglect in a way which not only aids understanding but also contributes to theories for helping, then we need clarity about whether what is needed is *knowledge* about nappy changing and the risk of nappy rash with its ensuing discomfort for the child or help in achieving a level of *emotional awareness* and connection with the child.

In this sense one link between attachment theory and neglect is the question mark over whether this is a cognitive or an emotional process – or whether, as David Howe (1993) has suggested, cognitive and emotional understanding between people are inseparable. The child develops an interest in the mental and emotional states of others. Knowing other minds and reading other's feelings are equally central to the child becoming part of the social world. This elaboration of the perspective taking ideas mentioned earlier, enables us to think about the nature of neglectful behaviour in rather a different way. The typical social work assessment of a family that is deemed to be neglectful would be likely to include the following statements:

- This mother is unable to understand and meet the needs of the child.
- This mother is unable to put the child's needs before her own.

The second statement is probably unhelpful in failing to acknowledge the constant process of negotiation about meeting the needs of all family members. However, perhaps if the parent is unable to know the mental and emotional state of the child and is also unable to allow the child access to her own mental and emotional state, the cycles which both build relationships and ensure children's needs are met will not go round. Thus the processes which enable the child to function in the social world are unlikely to be set up.

Understanding these processes may go some way to explaining why research has shown that children who have been neglected experience such extreme difficulties in all areas of development. Erickson et al. (1989) found that by the age of six, neglected children had dramatic difficulties at school both in terms of relationships and in terms of their ability to learn. In a number of tests they were found to experience more serious problems than physically abused or sexually abused children. It must be acknowledged that chronically inadequate care can lead to very severe developmental problems.

The concept of neglect is not in itself helpful without some idea of what specific area of parental care is being neglected and its impact on the child in the short and long term. This is equally true of physical neglect and emotional neglect. First it needs to be established, for example, what a necessary amount of food for a child of a particular age would be. The amount by which what this particular child consumed fell short of the necessary amount could then be calculated. Of course, the amount consumed by the child and the amount prepared by the mother and put on the child's plate may not be the same thing. From the point of view of the Children Act definition of significant harm, it could be said that if the child failed to gain weight within acceptable limits, then the child had suffered significant harm regardless of the circumstances and the parent was responsible because ensuring a child gains weight is a reasonable expectation of a parent. Finding a way of offering the parent support so that the right food both goes onto the plate and into the child in order for the child to gain weight requires an understanding of the more complex aspects of behaviour and relationships.

If we translate this analysis into a concern about emotional neglect, we can see that measuring what the mother put on the emotional plate, what was consumed by the child and what her 'weight', her emotional health, was at the end is an even tougher task. If we frame this emotional care by the parent in terms of attachment theory, then we would start with the whole range of measures of attachment followed up by an assessment of the cycles which make up the attachment process to see where the blocks are. From the literature on failure to thrive (Skuse 1994), we know that there is a complex equation involved in the process of giving and receiving food which has been underestimated. No-one would underestimate the difficulty of analysing what makes up the relationship of one human to another, and yet health and social work assessments have been dogged by the problem of whether child smiles equals happy, child cries equals sad, child smiles when sees mother at contact equals attachment equals good relationship and so on. Perhaps the dilemma is that however thorough the observation or assessment, the professional will only have a brief snapshot of what makes up the relationship between the adult and the child.

The link to parenting skills programmes

The comparison between physical care and emotional care is helpful partly because it highlights the sense in which certain aspects of parenting behaviour are more closely linked in the minds of professionals with the cognitive processes in the parent and the need for knowledge, whereas others are more closely linked with emotional warmth and the psychological well-being of the parent. Giving the baby regular feeds in a sterilised bottle may be in the first category. Behaving in an affectionate way towards a child may be in the second. Problems in either area may lead parents to be offered parenting skills training although demonstrating failure in the second without failure in the first would be less likely to attract attention unless it was an extreme case.

The very concept of training implies that problems in the parents' behaviour towards the child can be resolved by improving their knowledge base about parenthood and giving them the chance to assimilate these new ideas into their own behaviour. The curriculum currently used by social services departments is likely to cover a range of practical matters such as cooking and hygiene while also providing equally practical advice about giving the child stimulation, playing, giving the child praise and using certain strategies for discipline and control. The child's need for love and affection will be stressed but the assumption is often that this is a loving parent who lacks the necessary know-how to translate their feelings towards the child into the kind of behaviour that helps them to develop normally. In so far as the problem relates to a lack of knowledge, the solution is primarily a cognitive one. Failure to praise a child may be seen as a parent's failure to grasp that children need praise. The fact that the parent has not demonstrated their new knowledge by their behaviour leads to the conclusion that they have not 'learned'. When a programme of parenting skills training fails to achieve the hoped for change it is often seen as a lack of effort on the part of the parent. Rather as at school, the problem may be seen as 'must try harder'. If it is seen as a symptom of the parent's innate inability to learn, it is likely that further training may not be offered. In the absence of improvements in the care of the child and where the child's development is at risk of significant harm, this may lead to separation.

The difficulty for parenting skills programmes are many. First, they risk making a split between the emotional and the practical/behavioural aspects of parenting. Tymchuk and Andron (1990) in their work on the parenting skills of parents with learning disabilities, stress the practical elements. For example in their study, satisfactory child care was defined as:

the absence of complaints from the community as well as the positive evidence that the children were kept clean, adequately fed, clothed, and supervised, and attended school regularly.

It is not always clear on what basis the assessment has been made that at least the emotional relationship is good enough. Attachment theory has very little to say on the subject of parents 'loving' children, and whether the parent who loves a child will necessarily demonstrate Bowlby's sensitivity or Winnicott's maternal pre-occupation or will be making Fahlberg's cycles go round. Nevertheless it is likely that the quality of the parent's feeling for the child, however demonstrated to the clinician, will be seen as taking care of the emotional side of things.

Secondly, there is a tendency to forget the role of unconscious processes. As in other areas of social work practice, ignoring unconscious processes is bound to lead to an oversimplification. For instance, 'This mother loves her child but lacks knowledge about feeding and discipline. I will give her that knowledge and she will then be able to use it for herself.' I have recently heard a social worker say, 'I don't understand it. This mother can't communicate. I give her what she says she wants to help her look after her child and then she says she really wanted something else.' Is parenting behaviour really based on a careful weighing up of the options followed by a rational choice? We would not claim that for other areas of human behaviour and certainly our reactions as parents owe a good deal to a lifetime of different emotional

46

experiences and exposure to different ideas about ourselves and about children. Our ability to use knowledge must depend on a complex cocktail of past experiences and current stresses.

Which brings us to a further major factor, the varying levels of stress to which parents at stages in their lives are exposed. While the parents are being offered support to improve the care of the children, the circumstances of the family are likely to be constantly changing. For families living in poverty a small increase in the size of the electricity bill or a problem with the washing machine breaking can feel overwhelming. For women with limited social contacts and low self-esteem, a critical comment by a neighbour can produce a downward spiral in mood and energy levels, after which it may be hard to focus the mind on the strategy suggested by the family home help for coping with the wet beds and the temper tantrums. Unfortunately the children continue to experience going to bed in wet beds and also the parent's depression. Parents can sometimes be very aware of the distress of their children but are unable to relieve it.

These stresses are magnified for parents with learning disabilities who may be less able, for example, to tackle an unexpected debt and may also be even more vulnerable to isolation and stigma than other parents living in poverty. How do parenting programmes operate in this context? How does the quality of parent–child relationships earn a place on the curriculum?

Parents with learning disabilities – a special case?

The Children Act has put into legislation the principle which has long been part of good social work practice, that support services must be offered to families of children in need in order to ensure the opportunity for their children to achieve a satisfactory level of development (Children Act 1989 S.17). In order to meet that requirement, the particular needs of each family must be assessed. That assessment should derive from an understanding of children's developmental needs, including the need for attachment, and the kind of parental care which would meet those needs. A body of knowledge under these broad headings must then include the characteristics of those children who may have special developmental needs and the characteristics of those parents who may potentially have difficulties with certain aspects of parental care. Thus children with specific medical conditions or parents with mobility problems, for example, may have needs for certain kinds of services. A frequent complaint of those who advocate on behalf of parents with learning disabilities is that child care social workers have no training or experience in learning disabilities and are therefore not in a position to offer appropriate sources of help and support. There is ample evidence that parents with learning disabilities can be competent parents (Gath 1988, Tymchuk 1992). However there is a real difficulty for social workers, heath visitors and so on

47

in knowing how much weight to give the learning disability of a parent when working with families. In some cases there is a tendency to see the learning disability as the major factor in the parenting problems, rather than poor housing, for example. We know that all parents value and may need practical help. In other cases there is a tendency to offer help which pays little regard to the learning disability, perhaps by using written agreements which cannot be read let alone understood.

Booth and Booth (1994) would go further. They would argue that parents with learning disabilities are not only seriously disadvantaged by chronic financial, housing and social problems and may have experienced adversity in their own childhood. There is a danger that the statutory services will contribute to the stress already experienced by parents with learning disabilities and the extra pressure may contribute to rather than prevent family breakdown.

What is apparent is that there is a historical split between services for adults with disabilities and child care services and that this split tends to be reflected in the research literature. Booth and Booth take an adult-focused perspective in which they demand sensitivity to the difficulties faced by parents with learning disabilities. Powerful and important though their research is, they do not address situations where the needs of children are not being met in spite of the best efforts of parents and professional helpers.

Let us look briefly at what is known about the parenting capacity of parents with learning disabilities. There is a large body of research literature about parents with learning disabilities, which is probably better known to clinical psychologists than it is to social workers and other professional groups such as health visitors. This is not surprising, given that much of the research has been carried out by psychologists and psychiatrists who apply psychological research techniques and publish in their own journals. Much of this research into the parenting abilities of parents with learning disabilities, according to Dowdney and Skuse (1993), has failed to take into account the factors mentioned by Booth and Booth. Factors such as poverty, social isolation, history of abuse, violent partners – which people with learning disabilities are more likely to suffer from – are known to be associated with family stress, abuse and neglect. What is more, the assessments of parenting which are used both to demonstrate the problems of parents with learning disabilities and then to measure the success of programmes to assist them are often based on brief observations in a clinical setting.

Dowdney and Skuse conclude that the research literature on intervention programmes is also inconclusive and inadequate. Some studies demonstrate improvements with families where abuse or neglect has occurred but other research suggests a very poor prognosis. The majority of studies agree that parents with learning disabilities have problems generalising acquired skills to new situations. This includes changes in the child's developmental level.

It is helpful to look at examples of the research in more detail. Given my earlier comparison between learning how to feed a child appropriately and learning how to respond appropriately emotionally, a similar comparison is possible in the research on interventions. Sarber et al. (1983) were able to demonstrate that they could teach a mother with a learning disability, who had previously neglected her child, how to provide nutritious food. The mother was able to generalise this skill to the home setting. In contrast, Tymchuk and Andron (1988) used a programme to teach parents to restrict the use of physical punishment and increase praise. Although there were some gains in these two specific areas, there was little improvement in spontaneous positive affect, and a persisting lack of ability to apply rules flexibly to meet their children's developmental needs. Areas of parenting which require sensitivity to the child rather than following rules appear to be more difficult to change. Booth and Booth (1994: 21) argue:

> Support is more effective when directed to the survival needs of families, followed by child care tasks, than to modifying styles of interaction within the family.

This may well be true and one could argue that practical help can relieve emotional pressures also. But it begs the question of whether, where styles of interaction continue to cause upset to children and parents in spite of the provision of practical help, we should be looking for more effective ways of responding.

It seems likely from the research available that parents with learning disabilities are vulnerable to parenting problems for the same range of personal, economic and social reasons as other parents. This vulnerability is increased by the fact that their learning disability makes it more difficult for them to find their way through the obstacle course of life on limited incomes or in a situation of exploitation by a partner. Because of their life experiences, when parents with learning disabilities have such severe problems with their children that the children's development is significantly impaired, it may be difficult for professionals to work in partnership and to bring about change. Some of these blocks may be in the parents, since research suggests that it can be harder for parents with learning disabilities to learn more appropriate ways of caring physically and responding emotionally to their children. They may also feel very anxious about the involvement of powerful agencies and may swing between on the one hand being hostile and on the other hand being almost too compliant. But many of the blocks are in the professional network which may focus on incapacity rather than capacity and see the learning disability as an insuperable barrier.

One of the features of the research which is commented on by Tymchuk (1992) is the lack of attention which has been paid to the emotional development of children of parents with learning disabilities. The focus has been very much on the cognitive development of children, where the concerns about

49

limited stimulation by parents are complicated by concerns about whether the children may also have inherited learning difficulties. However the links via attachment theory between cognitive and emotional development are still to be taken into account.

McGaw and Sturmey (1994) have developed their own model for assessment and intervention with parents with learning disabilities. What they call the Parental Skills Model (See Figure 3.3) emphasises the connections between different aspects of the parents' history and current circumstances and these are linked with the developmental status of the child. The model is an attempt to bring together the research by psychologists like Tymchuk, Andron, Feldman and so on with material on child development and Department of Health Guidelines on assessment and child protection.

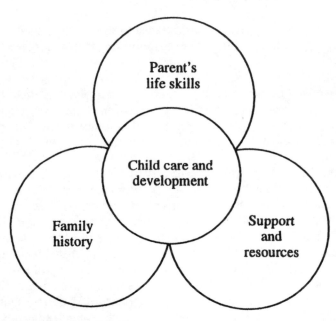

Figure 3.3 Parental skills model
(McGaw and Sturmey 1994)

McGaw and Sturmey's model of assessment places greater emphasis on problems in relationships both as a source of problems for the child and as a focus for intervention. The authors believe on the basis of research such as that by Crittenden and Bonvillian (1984) and Feldman et al. (1985) that there may be differences in the quality of parent–child interactions between some mothers with mild learning disabilities and their children. Sturmey and McGaw conclude, specifically, that some learning disabled mothers are 'less likely to show affection, stimulate and bond with their child in contrast to mothers who do not have learning disabilities'. We need to be very cautious before attributing the relationship difficulties exclusively to the learning disability but continue to explore the nature of those difficulties and the experiences of the parents.

In specific problem areas, such as dealing with disruptive behaviour in a child, the fact that parents with learning disabilities may be more likely to react punitively and find it hard to see anything good in the child's behaviour is seen as a lack of knowledge which can be dealt with by referral to parenting skills training. This is acknowledged to be an area which needs further investigation, not least in establishing the consequences for the child of this kind of treatment by a parent (Tymchuk and Andron 1990). This form of punitive parenting would normally be seen to have links with low self-esteem in children and if it was the dominant style of parenting not compensated by other positive experiences from parents, may well be seen as emotional abuse or neglect.

If we return now to the model described earlier in which parenting, attachment and developmental needs are linked, we can start to think about the dilemmas facing parents with learning disabilities. Booth and Booth (1994) quote Schilling et al. (1982) :

They tend to be disadvantaged in each of the three main ways that most people learn about childrearing: direct experience, observation and reading.

When we think about parenting in this way, it raises the question of whether parenting is different from other relationships. Do we learn how to parent or does the good enough parent build the relationship with the child in a way that reflects the parent's relational style, perhaps in effect their emotional health? There is an unresolved question about whether a minimum level of emotional health in the parent is necessary before benefiting from any parenting programme. This is a dilemma in working with many families. Given the trauma in the background of the parents with learning disabilities who cause concern, I speculate that there may be a sense in which their difficulty in making sense of their own experiences adds to the cognitive/emotional mix they bring to parenting. Recent research into the attachment experiences of adults suggests that adults' ability to understand and reflect on their own relationships with attachment figures has an impact on the quality of their relationships with their children. Even where early experiences have been unsatisfactory, if parents can make sense of them and talk coherently about them, this appears to be a protective factor (Main 1991). Early experiences of harm will not necessarily predict parenting problems but it needs to be taken into account when offering help.

51

Case example

The purpose of this case example, which has been appropriately disguised, is to demonstrate the way in which concerns about the development of the children and the quality of the parenting often centre on emotional and behavioural problems while the help which is offered tends to focus on practical skills. The parent's learning disability is seen as the main cause for the difficulties but it is unclear what the links are between the relationship problems and the learning disability.

The Jackson family

Mrs Jackson first came to the attention of the social services department as a pregnant sixteen year old who had recently left a local special school. During the next ten years she had three children and each in turn caused such high levels of concern that notwithstanding intensive support and work of various kinds with Mrs Jackson, they were all removed and placed in permanent substitute care. This then is an extremely sad case but the pattern of events is not wholly exceptional.

Mrs Jackson was one of three children who had been placed in the care of another authority by their parents when Mrs Jackson was two years old. The children lived in three separate foster homes and had some contact with their parents. They were reunited with their parents when Mrs Jackson was about thirteen years old. At one stage she had been in a school for children with severe learning difficulties but had transferred to a school for children with moderate learning difficulties when she was fourteen years old. Much of this information is very hazy and comes from other family members. When interviewed in her twenties, Mrs Jackson remembered nothing of her childhood before the age of fourteen. She seemed unable to think about or describe how her relationship with adult carers had been. She had married the father of the younger two children but that relationship had broken down and she received almost no assistance from him.

In order to make sense of a long history of concerns about the children, stress for the family and uncertainties in the professional network, I am proposing to look at the issues at a particular point in time for the younger two of Mrs Jackson's three children, the first child having been adopted when he was a baby following an assault by a male partner and neglect by Mrs Jackson. What I hope to highlight are the specific developmental problems of the children, the parenting behaviours of the mother and the difficulties involved in assessment and planning.

Mark and Darren Jackson

Mark (aged six) and his younger brother, Darren (aged two) were accommodated at the request of their mother who had been saying for some time that she felt unable to cope and had finally snapped and hit Mark quite hard across the face. The social services and health visiting services had all been involved at intervals over the previous eight years and at this stage it was the school who were most concerned about Mark. The assessments had to focus on the different developmental needs of the two children and their mother's ability to meet them. The quality of the relationship in terms of attachment was also a factor to be considered, although this was not spelled out specifically by the agencies involved.

Mark was having problems in almost all areas of his development at the time of admission to foster care. Emotionally, he appeared to be looking for relationships with any adult who showed him kindness but was unable to be close to his mother, with whom he had endless battles. At home, he had been spending a lot of time locked in his bedroom. At school, he was unable to follow a normal timetable and attacked staff on a daily basis, seriously kicking and hitting out. This behaviour had led to staff going to the hospital casualty department on occasion. There were other developmental concerns. His language development had been poor and although of normal intelligence, he had very poor concentration. Socially, he could respond appropriately to adults and children, but if something upset him he would erupt with uncontrollable rage and obvious panic. He had a very low self-esteem and assumed nobody liked him. He had no sense of emotional containment and he seemed to disintegrate when under stress.

Although there had been long-standing concerns about the fact that Mark was understimulated and out of control, there was apparently nothing in the records relating to his first two to three years which would predict the level of disturbance which he showed at the age of six years. The almost daily visits from family centre workers, health visitors and family home helps had apparently done nothing to halt the steady deterioration in the relationship between Mrs Jackson and Mark. While these workers were present, the children received warmth and stimulation from the helpers and the mother herself was able to play a little – but the mother–child relationship continued to deteriorate. Mrs Jackson saw Mark as a naughty child who deliberately upset her and was too powerful. He did his best to keep his distance from her physically and emotionally, but his compulsive, repetitious behaviours such as constantly switching the television or radio on and off, attracted her anger.

At the time the children were accommodated, Mrs Jackson said that she was not able to control Mark and did not feel able to have him home again. She did want Darren to return home once she had had a break. It was extremely difficult to assess the likely future for Darren. At two years old, he was demonstrating all the same features as Mark had done at the same age. He was also out of control and developmentally delayed. However, as Mark had been, he was often smiley and seemed affectionate towards his mother. His mother was reacting in the same way to Darren as she had to Mark at that age. She could talk affectionately of Darren still, which she no longer could of Mark, but she felt that his behaviour was a deliberate attack on her and that he was now showing his true colours as a 'naughty boy'. As before, she co-operated with the visits from professionals, but seemed unable to apply the lessons or would apply them inflexibly, leaving Mark and Darren in their bedrooms or in the hallway for long periods and creating extreme anxiety and confusion by erratic, incongruent behaviour; shouting while smiling, 'play fighting' while telling them not to hit her, telling them to stop certain behaviour but if they did, threatening to punish them anyway.

It seemed that Mrs Jackson was unable to keep the children 'in mind'. If she put Darren's lunch in front of him in his high chair in the kitchen, she would sit in the living room until Darren threw the dish on the floor and Mark came to tell her about it. If Mark was in the hallway as a punishment, she would find it difficult to appreciate his feelings about that, particularly if he had no idea why he was there. The children gradually learned that they must bring their needs to her attention as a matter of urgency, because she would not be able to anticipate them.

The package of parenting skills offered by the social services department focused on learning about the needs of children. The practical advice which she received about the nutrition of the children confused her. It was suggested that she try to home cook all their food, including items such as meat pies, and she was told not to go to the chip shop any more. She was not very angry about such expectations but felt set apart from her family and neighbours. She liked the family home help who came to the shops with her and wanted to show she was a good mother. However, the children had constant diarrhoea and this caused further concern.

Although some attention was paid to the need for the mother to praise the children more, the emphasis on the need to control the children and set limits, arising primarily from the mother's own concerns and professional fears for the children's safety, added to the distance between mother and children and increased the negative content of the parent–child interactions. The sessions decreased rather than increased her confidence and the children's reactions to the professional helpers reminded her of her failures.

On the whole, the mother never stopped feeling that Mark and probably Darren were as they were and no amount of 'work' would change them. Similarly, she felt that 'being backward' meant that she would never be able to change herself either. Her continuing lack of connection with Mark and the start of a similar decline in Darren's experience of her, defeated everyone.

Darren did return to his mother's care but within a short space of time his behaviour deteriorated to the point where his mother had to use reins to tie him to furniture in the house in order to control him. He has since been placed in foster care.

If we look at this situation from an attachment perspective, we see that the mother's own history is one of loss and separation. The mother's inability to talk about or apparently remember her own childhood and attachment figures may be of concern (Main 1991). Although it appears that she was able to establish some degree of reciprocity with the children as babies, this appeared to be because she knew that babies were helpless and needed her to feed them. They were then rewarding to her. As babies became toddlers, she was unable to accept their needs as legitimate. Using Fahlberg's cycles it is clear that the mother was finding it very difficult to meet their needs once those needs reflected children who wanted to assert themselves, make choices and explore their world. Because their needs were not getting met, the cycle (see Figure 3.1: The arousal–relaxation cycle) was getting blocked and the children remained in a state of high arousal. In this situation, the cycle is not completed by the adult meeting the child's needs. The child does not build trust and attachment but instead learns to release the tension through destructive means. High arousal can lead to an aggressive outburst which may result in rejection or physical punishment. The child may reach a state of relaxation but the lesson learned about relationships is one of lack of trust .

For Mrs Jackson, initiating positive interactions also became increasingly difficult as the children got older, again largely because she felt that she had a very fragile control of them and was unable to take the risk of rejection. To use the Fahlberg positive interaction cycle, the children therefore failed to develop self-esteem. The absence of a secure base, to use Bowlby's terms, meant that all the children's energy was tied up in anxiety about proximity to their mother. Such children are unable to learn and become stuck in terms of their own cognitive as well as emotional development. It is not surprising that for many children like Mark, it is at school that the full extent of their problems emerges.

Although there were some serious problems for the children and the attachment relationship with their mother was insecure, there were signs that they had experienced some satisfactory emotional care at some early stage. They were still looking for a good relationship and responded well to adults who seemed to offer a special relationship. Mark, for example, became very devoted to the voluntary driver who took him to school. In Fahlberg's terms, the boys were at least expressing needs and allowing adults to meet them.

The attachment difficulties contributed to the children being very demanding and unrewarding. It was impossible to turn the situation around by giving Mrs Jackson information about diet or teaching her how to play and indeed workers were frustrated by the lack of progress in these areas. Given the mother's troubled history it may not have been possible to intervene in order to successfully build relationships between this mother and her children. Mark was almost too late to help in the sense that he was already too disturbed to cope in a normal school environment. How could Darren's future have been different?

Changes in the mother may be such a long term process that the children are not able to wait. What does seem to emerge from such a history is that interventions must target the emotional relationship as well as the physical care at a very early stage, if a child's healthy development is to be fostered. They also need to occur within a preventive programme. Perhaps the time when life is going well for the family may be the best time to help parents prepare for the next stage, rather than close the case. We are still better at using attachment theory for understanding when things go wrong. There needs now to be an effort to integrate such theories for understanding into theories for helping, not as an alternative for practical help and support or parent education, but as a way of acknowledging that without developing trust and self-esteem, children like Mark and Darren are not able to learn and grow and mothers like Mrs Jackson face another tragic loss.

Conclusions

For families where there is a concern about neglect, there will always be a need to give consideration to the quality of the emotional relationship. The welcome new demands for increased family support will not be effective unless the emotional life of children and parents is taken into account. Attachment theory gives us a way of thinking about this and more needs to be done to devise strategies for repairing relationships. Professionals working with parents with learning disabilities too often become so pre-occupied with what is seen as a lack of knowledge of children's needs, particularly in the areas of diet and discipline, that the attachment relationship does not receive the attention it should. Although knowledge of attachment theory has been around for decades, it has been more widely used as an aspect of assessment, and even then not always fully understood. Parental skills training must be adapted to give greater focus to the quality of the emotional relationship, so that parents can share their complex feelings about their child and the child's emotional development can become a central aim of the work.

References

Boddy, J.M. and Skuse, D.H. (1994) 'The process of parenting in failure to thrive' *Journal of Child Psychology and Psychiatry* 35(3): 401–425

Booth, T. and Booth,W. (1994) *Parenting under Pressure: Mothers and Fathers with Learning Difficulties.* Buckingham: Open University Press

Bowlby, J. (1969) *Attachment and Loss, Volume 1: Attachment.* London: Hogarth Press.

Bowlby, J. (1982) (2nd edition) *Attachment and Loss, Volume 1: Attachment.* London: Hogarth Press.

Bowlby, J. (1988) *A Secure Base: Clinical Applications of Attachment Theory.* London: Routledge.

Children Act (1989) HMSO.

Crittenden, P.M. and Bonvillien, J.D. (1984) 'The relationship between maternal risk status and maternal sensitivity'. *American Orthopsychiatric Association* 54: 250–262.

Crittenden, P.M. and Ainsworth, M.D.S. (1989) 'Child Maltreatment and Attachment Theory', in Cicchetti, D. and Carlson, V. (eds) *Child Maltreatment: Theory and Research on the Causes and Consequences of Child Abuse and Neglect.* New York: Cambridge University Press.

Dowdney, L. and Skuse, D. (1993) 'Parenting provided by adults with a mental retardation.' *Journal of Child Psychology and Psychiatry* 34(1): 25–47.

Erickson, M.F., Egeland, B. and Pianta, R. (1989) ' The Effects of Maltreatment on the Development of Young Children', in Cicchetti, D. and Carlson, V. (eds) *Child Maltreatment: Theory and Research on the Causes and Consequences of Child Abuse and Neglect.* New York: Cambridge University Press.

Fahlberg, V. (1988) *Fitting the Pieces Together.* London: BAAF.

Fahlberg, V. (1991) *A Child's Journey Through Placement* London: BAAF.

Feldman, M.A., Case, L., Towns, F. and Betel, J. (1985) 'Parent education project: development and nurturance of children of mentally retarded parents.' *American Journal of Mental Deficiency* 90: 253–258.

Gath, A. (1988) 'Mentally handicapped people as parents. Is mental retardation a bar to adequate parenting?' *Journal of Child Psychology and Psychiatry* 29: 739–744.

Gesell, A, Halverson, H.M., Ilg, F.L. and Thompson, H. (1940) *The First Five Years of Life: The Preschool Years* New York: Harper and Row.

Howe, D. (1993) *On Being a Client.* London: Sage.

McGaw, S. and Sturmey, P. (1994) 'Assessing parents with learning disabilities'. *Child Abuse Review* 3: 36–51.

Main, M. (1991) 'Metacognitive knowledge, metacognitive monitoring, and singular (coherent) vs. multiple (incoherent) model of attachment: Findings and directions for future research.' in Parkes, C.M., Stevenson-Hinde, J. and Marris, P. *Attachment across the Life Cycle* London: Routledge.

Sarber, R.E., Halasz, M.M., Messmer, M.C., Bickett, A.D. and Lutzker, J.R. (1983) 'Teaching menu planning and grocery shopping skills to a mentally retarded mother'. *Mental Retardation,* 21: 101–106.

Schilling, R., Schinke, S., Blythe, B. and Bath, R. (1982) 'Child maltreatment and mentally retarded parents:is there a relationship?' *Mental Retardation* 20(5): 201–209.

Tymchuk, A. (1992) 'Predicting adequacy of parenting by parents with mental retardation'. *Child Abuse and Neglect* 16: 165–178.

Tymchuk, A.J. and Andron, L. (1988) 'Clinic and home parent training of a mother with mental handicap caring for three children with developmental delay. *Mental Handicap Research,* (1): 24–38.

Tymchuk, A. and Andron, L. (1990) 'Mothers with mental retardation who do or do not abuse or neglect their children." *Child Abuse and Neglect,* 14: 313–423.

Winnicott, D.W. (1965) *The Maturational Process and the Facilitating Environment* New York: International Universities Press.

4   Attachment reviewed through a cultural lens

Stephen Parvez Rashid

> There are three conditions which often look alike yet differ completely,
> flourish in the same hedgerow:
> Attachment to self and to things and to persons, detachment
> From self and from things and from persons, and growing between them,
> indifference
> Which resembles the others as death resembles life,
> Being between two lives – unflowering, between
> The live and the dead nettle.
> > T.S. Eliot: *Four Quartets* – 'Little Gidding' (1944) III lines 1–7

The sentiments underlying these striking lines appear to have prompted little attention from developmental psychologists in general and from attachment theorists in particular. Most writers on attachment would take issue with Eliot's description of attachment as a 'condition', since it is generally characterised otherwise. Thus Bretherton (1985) writes about 'the attachment system' whose purpose is 'to regulate behaviours designed to maintain or obtain proximity to and contact with . . . the attachment figures' (ibid p.6) who in turn provide(s) the attached person with 'felt security' (Bischof 1975). The focus of interest is on the process of attachment, which develops out of the relationship between a young child and his/her primary caregivers within the first year of the child's life. Bretherton notes that:

> attachment behaviour tends to be most obvious, when the attached person is frightened, fatigued or sick and is assuaged when the attachment figure provides protection, help and soothing . . . Finally, although attachment behaviour is most noticeable in early childhood, it can be observed throughout the life cycle, especially in stressful situations. (ibid p.6)

Bretherton's account summarises the views of Bowlby (1982) which are explored in greater detail and extended in her review article. Her language is very different from Eliot's, being rooted in a scientific psychological discourse in marked contrast to his poetical discourse. Indeed one could argue that they are interested in very different aspects of the same phenomenon, she in the *process* and he in the *outcomes* of that process as experienced by different individuals. Eliot's three 'conditions' may thus be seen as possible stances by an adult person towards the world, that is an individual's *Weltanschauung*. Furthermore these embrace a wider range of phenomena than usually considered by attachment theorists, 'things' as well as 'self' and 'persons'. It is also noteworthy that since the seminal work of Bowlby (1982) and Ainsworth (1967, 1972) much attention has been paid to attachment, rather less has been written about 'detachment' as a positive response to the world or about 'indifference' as a defence against that world. The image of attachment as 'the live nettle' in the hedgerow is a potent one, carrying connotations of discomfort and pain, yet also flowering and hence fruitful, unlike indifference.

Of Eliot's three conditions, attachment provides the focus for this chapter. It will argue that attachment, like other universal phenomena is nevertheless patterned and shaped by its cultural context. Evidence will be cited from anthropology and cultural psychology for the impact of cultural norms on comparative child development. Arising from this the issue of multiple caregivers is considered, since attachment theory has traditionally emphasised the importance of a single primary caregiver. The impact of cultural norms on some psychoanalytical writing is briefly reviewed via the writing of Kakar (1990) and Doi (1962, 1990), especially since the latter's formulation of the concept of *amae* has been utilised by attachment researchers in the Japanese context (Miyake et al. 1985). This leads to an examination of studies of attachment in other cultures, namely Uganda (Ainsworth 1967 and 1977), Germany (Grossmann et al. 1985), Israel (Sagi et al. 1985) and Japan (Miyake et al. 1985 Takahashi 1986). The finding that *intracultural* variations in attachment patterns may be larger than crosscultural ones (Van IJzendoorn and Kroonenberg 1988) directs attention to disadvantaged groups within a particular society and leads to literature on African–American groups (Barbarin 1993), which argues strongly for the importance of contextual factors, particularly poverty and racism, in affecting child development. Maternal attachment and child survival in conditions of extreme socioeconomic hardship are then examined through the powerfully moving account of Scheper-Hughes (1990, 1992) writing in the context of north east Brazil. The chapter concludes with considerations for practice in contemporary British society which is multi-cultural and multi-racial.

A universal concept and its shaping

Few would argue with the assertion that attachment is a universal phenomenon which may be observed in human beings, in other mammals and in avian species. It thus has biological and physiological roots as well as psychological ones (see Hinde 1982, 1991). However, universal phenomena in the human world are mediated through symbolic structures of language, context and meaning before they can be understood and John Berger reminds us that:

to try to understand the experience of another, it is necessary to dismantle the world as seen from one's own place within it, and to reassemble it as seen from his. (Berger 1975)

The argument of this chapter is that attachment, like bereavement, is shaped or patterned by the culture within which it takes place. It is widely accepted that the universal phenomenon of bereavement is experienced very differently, according to the rites, beliefs and customs of the society in which it occurs. Thus, while the English language retains the phrase 'sackcloth and ashes' from the mourning rites described in the Old Testament, the act of donning sackcloth or rubbing ash into one's hair as an expression of grief would evoke surprise, dismay and even alarm in contemporary British society. Only if the mourner was clearly identified with Jewish, Muslim or other minority communities within Britain, where such practice was customary, would this behaviour be considered normal. Even so it is all too possible for the mourner's behaviour to be labelled as 'abnormal' or 'pathological'. Bavington (1980) describes how a grieving Pakistani woman in Bradford was referred by her English G.P. for compulsory psychiatric admission to hospital when her culturally normal behaviour whilst mourning a revered uncle was mistaken for mental illness (see also Wilks 1990). A wholly unnecessary and potentially damaging psychiatric admission was avoided only because a key professional, in this case the psychiatrist, was able to locate the behaviour properly in its cultural context and to recognise its meaning for the individual concerned and for those around her. The lessons for practice from this case example are clear and directly transferable from the example of bereavement to attachment. If both these phenomena, and the behaviours which accompany them, are shaped by their cultural context, it becomes crucial for practising professionals to recognise this explicitly in order to make accurate assessments and avoid mistakes like the one committed by the Bradford G.P. It would be all too easy for child care professionals to attempt to evaluate the strength and nature of the attachment relationship between children and care-givers by using culturally specific notions like direct eye contact, for example, in settings where this might be regarded as culturally inappropriate (see below for further discussion). This becomes particularly important when the professionals' own cultural norms and expectations are markedly different from those of the children and care givers. Therefore practitioners need to be aware of their own cultural norms, and those that underpin their professional judgements, as well as the cultural norms of their clients.

The cultural patterning of infant behaviour

Evidence has accumulated from anthropologists and from cultural psychologists that cultural norms in different societies shape child development. An often cited example is of parent–infant gaze or eye contact. Brazelton (1977) noted that amongst the Mayan Indians of Mexico, mothers made few attempts to engage their infants' attention by talking or face-to-face interaction. The Gusii people of South Western Kenya have been extensively studied by American anthropologists and developmental child psychologists at Harvard University (Dixon et al. 1981, Richman 1983, Richman et al. 1988, LeVine 1990) and have been compared with an American sample of upper middle class suburban families from Boston, Massachusetts. One striking finding is the consistent discouragement by Gusii mothers of direct eye contact with their infants. In Gusii terms direct gaze is associated with disrespect, and discouragement of this 'helps to maintain the hierarchial order of the home' (LeVine 1990 p.461). Such a view is not restricted to the Gusii. It would certainly be familiar to children from the Indian subcontinent, that to show respect to one's parents, elders and authority figures like teachers, it is customary to avert one's eyes. Anecdotal evidence suggests that British teachers in the 1960s and 1970s were puzzled by the reluctance of Indian and Pakistani school children, especially girls, to look at them when spoken to. Doubtless those children were even more puzzled by exhortations from exasperated teachers to 'Look at me when I speak to you!' How could a teacher be commanding a pupil to behave so rudely?

In the Gusii example, however, there are more complex reasons for avoiding direct gaze. A Gusii mother who gives her child the visual (and verbal) attention common amongst American mothers is not only taking pride and pleasure in her child (to paraphrase LeVine 1990) she is inviting the destructiveness of others who may be jealous of her good fortune and therefore attempt through witchcraft to spoil that good fortune. For the same reasons Gusii parents did not praise their children's academic, verbal or motor achievements. Indeed, in comparison to American children the Gusii children appeared understimulated, under-achieving and generally more passive. In Gusii terms, however, social cohesion and stability are far more important than individual achievement and therefore the purpose of traditional child-rearing practices are well suited to the values of that society. Thus the *meaning* of parent–child gaze is embedded in societal values and cannot be understood without the cultural context.

Bretherton (1985) makes a similar point when she discusses two anthropological accounts of contrasting communities, the Tikopia in Micronesia who were studied by Firth in the 1920s, and a Balinese village community in Indonesia described by Bateson and Mead in 1942. Both studies therefore predate the formulation of attachment theory. Firth quotes one of the chiefs of the Tikopia as follows:

The child knows its own mother and its own father also by tokens – it looks constantly on them. The infant recognizes its parents while it yet cannot speak. Faces only are recognised; therefore when it looks then on faces which are different, the infant cries. The babe which has not yet made speech [i.e. begun to speak properly], if its father be absent, be he gone to the woods or hither for a stroll, it seeks then for its father, cries, cries, cries, calling 'Pa! Pa E! Pa E! Pa, pa, pa, pa!' That is, it knows the relatives, but it weeps for its father. When they listen to it, crying 'pa, pa, pa, pa' thereupon someone goes out to look for him. When the father is found he asks 'What?' 'Come to the child who has cried and cried for you; cried Pa awfully!' Thereupon its father goes over, lifts it upon his arms, and so looking at its father it stops and does not cry. And the infant scolds its father, 'You went-went-went-went!' (Firth 1936, p.157)

It is easy to recognise the elements of attachment theory in this account. It is interesting to note that Firth was initially sceptical of such accounts but his own observations persuaded him that they were accurate. Bretherton (1985) notes that the Tikopia were concerned that the child's attachment to parents did not become too exclusive, but was extended by interaction to important relatives who became secondary care-givers and provided strong supportive relationships into adult life (Firth 1936). By contrast the Balinese community used parent–child interactions and, in Bretherton's terminology, the attachment system, to very different ends. By simulating fear, mothers sought to control their infants' movements, calling out 'Beware of wild cats/caterpillars etc.' where there were none. Infants who did not necessarily understand the words heeded the emotional tone of voice and were checked. In this community mothers also 'teased' their infants, engaging them in play and then 'looking away' with a blank look. This led to outbursts of temper and sulking by infants who were presumably baffled by the sudden ceasing of the playful interaction. Bateson and Mead (1942) report that by the time the children were 2–3 years old they ceased to pay any attention to such playful interaction. Bretherton (1985) comments that 'one has the strong impression that the children were being trained not to respond to provocation, to disengage emotional expression from emotional experience, a valued ability among the Balinese' (p.28).

In these two examples, argues Bretherton, 'the functioning of the attachment system is moulded by different cultural ideas and beliefs' (op.cit p.28). She concludes that from a universalist point of view the Tikopian pattern might be regarded as 'a more optimal ontogenetic adaptation' that is, better, but from a culturally relative perspective both patterns are 'ontogenetically adaptive' in their own terms, that is, they are well suited to meeting the needs of their own particular society. This has led Hinde (1982) to argue in Bretherton's words that 'What is *best* must be considered against the whole background of family, social groups and cultural beliefs. A mother–child relation that produces successful adults in one situation will not necessarily do so in another' (Bretherton 1985 p.25). Hence a child brought up in the Balinese tradition described by Bateson and Meade would have some difficulty, one might suppose, adapting to Tikopian society, and vice versa. To pursue the point with the earlier example of the Gusii, Quinton (1994) has argued that the behaviour developed by their traditional child rearing, and the values which underpin them, 'become increasingly problematic as the culture accommodates to modern pressures' and 'as the requirements for a well adapted adult change' (p.176).

Single parent attachment vs. multiple mothering

The prominence given in much writing on attachment to a single mother or mother-figure can be traced to Freud's statement describing the child's relationship to its mother as 'unique, without parallel, established unalterably for a whole lifetime as the first and strongest love-object and as the prototype of all later love relations – for both sexes' (Freud 1940, p.188). Bowlby's (1958) principle of monotropy reinforced this view by implying that the mother figure becomes the *principal* attachment figure and that all other attachment figures are secondary. Although Bowlby later revised his view, the notion has persisted strongly, both amongst professionals and in the literature (e.g. Sluckin et al. 1983) that the mother figure is or should be the primary attachment figure. It has even been argued by Blurton-Jones (1972) and by Konner (1977) that there is a *biological* basis to preference for a single mother-figure, since this occurs in hunter-gatherer societies, which are seen as prototypical of all subsequent societies. Consequently the notion that multiple mothering can be a satisfactory or better alternative is viewed with considerable scepticism, even disbelief. Thus Quinton (1994) has noted that 'in the West multiple mothering in early infancy is often associated with abnormal psychosocial development' (p.176), and Kareem (1992), writing as a psychotherapist, makes a very similar point.

However, studies by Tronick et al. (1987) and Morelli and Tronick (1991) of the Efe pygmies of the Ituri Forest in Zaire show clearly that hunter-gatherer societies which have developed multiple mothering of infants from birth onwards can and do produce sociable, co-operative adults. In Efe society the belief that it is harmful for a new born infant to be held first by its mother leads to a group of women attending the birth and passing the newborn infant around the group to be suckled by them. This multiple feeding and mothering continues and Tronick et al. observed that at eighteen weeks infants spent on average 60% of their time in physical contact with women other than their mothers. Thus the basic needs were met communally in a stable group of caretakers of which the mother was part. Quinton (1994) comments that 'in this case the parenting pattern was part of a different child-rearing ecology

64

compared with the West, where multiple caretaking often reflects a *failure* in the child-care system' (p.177 emphasis original). Kareem (1992) notes that:

> it is not uncommon for many white professionals to find it difficult to understand the implications of the family patterns in African and West Indian families. In their bewilderment it is also not uncommon for such therapists to make comments such as 'This child must have been damaged by the multiple relationships of the mother or father. There is little I can do' or 'Brought up by grandparents – why? What were the parents doing?' 'If the children have joined their parents here – in the U.K. – at such a late stage what can you expect but very disturbed behaviour?' (p.29)

Responses of this nature are not simply unhelpful, they are damaging and undermining of the client. They presuppose that the particular pattern of childrearing or mothering which is familiar to the professionals is universally 'ontologically adaptive'. They thereby devalue the clients' different pattern of childcare and implicitly, or perhaps explicitly, blame the clients for whatever difficulties are being experienced. In so doing white professionals are expressing their own inadequacy in comprehending the situation and hence their inability to intervene effectively.

Kareem warns that if British professionals, including workers in childcare, 'remain set in their belief that what matters most is encompassed in their own idea of family and child-rearing, then other mothers and carers with their own ideas are placed in an inferior position' (ibid p.29). This provides an excellent example of 'cultural imperialism' by Eurocentric professionals, no less damaging for being unwitting and all the harder to counter for being rooted in sincerely held beliefs about the primacy of attachment to a single mother figure. These beliefs can be challenged by the sort of example provided by Kareem of 'a highly educated and intelligent (African) man, working as an expert for an international agency' who described 'with great joy and emotion that he was loved and cared for by thirteen different mothers, his father's wives and partners, and said with much warmth 'it was not just one pair of hands or one pair of breasts that continuously fed me, cuddled me and cared for me. I was a prince among princes' (ibid p.30). Far from being inferior, abnormal or pathological, such an experience of child-rearing, not unlike that of the Efe people, would appear to have much to recommend it, and one can only agree that any child growing up like Kareem's client is indeed fortunate.

Fernandez (1991) cites Indian examples of multiple mothering (p.104) and contrasts the difference between Western and Indian patterns in the words of an Indian respondent to Murphy (1953): 'You bring up your children, we live with ours'. Fernandez questions 'the heavy emphasis on the mother (or surrogate)/child derived from Bowlby's work' which, she maintains, 'makes little sense in cultures where multiple carers are the norm' (ibid p.112), as for instance in India and amongst Indian communities outside the subcontinent.

She appears to be directly criticising Sluckin, Herbert and Sluckin (1983). Writing for an Australian audience she argues for a cultural relativist approach as Australian society 'becomes increasingly multi-cultural and more involved in relations with the Asian Pacific region'. She emphasises 'the importance of recognising that people define things differently and that the practices and beliefs of any group must always be evaluated within the cultural context in which they occur' (ibid p.113). She cites Jamrozik's concern that in the area of child abuse and neglect the cultural context is frequently ignored and that problems are frequently perceived in 'the perspective of the dominant cultural and professional monism' (Jamrozik 1986). Jamrozik gives the example of an older child from a minority ethnic group being asked to look after younger siblings while the parents are out as one where the dominant white Australian norms may see the caretaker sibling as abused or neglected and Fernandez makes the point that in many non-western cultures sibling caretaking 'is seen as an important antecedent to nurturant, responsible behaviour' (ibid p.114).

Ambert (1994) notes that 'to some extent one encounters multiple parenting among African–Americans and even more so in some Caribbean communities' (p.531) as well as in traditional Polynesian cultures. Citing the work of Collins (1992), Hunter and Ensminger (1992) and Ritchie and Ritchie (1981) in support of her statement, she makes the important point that when members of such societies migrate to societies where very different norms prevail, then 'this situation becomes aberrant' and 'multiple parenting becomes 'dysfunctional' for several reasons: the children are caught between two traditions; the urban environments into which families have moved are often more dangerous than the original environment where multiple parenting was practised, and child welfare professionals stigmatize the mothers for their apparent negligence. Ambert concludes her discussion of multiple parenting by stating that 'these modes of parenting place a serious question mark on much of the literature that emphasises the necessity for a child to have only one adult attachment figure, usually the mother, in order to mature normally . . . The notion of parents, especially of mothers, as the necessary source of children's current and later personal stability does not hold cross-culturally, nor for that matter, historically' (ibid p.531).

Universal process and cultural mediation – two examples from psychoanalysis

The extent to which psychoanalytic writers have considered the influence of cultural factors is not very great. It is worth noting, however, that in this context the Freudian notion of the Oedipus complex received some attention. An early example is afforded by Malinowski, who undertook anthropological fieldwork amongst the Trobriand Islanders in the South Pacific during

66

1914–18. He was struck by the matrilineal nature of Trobriand society, and he therefore argued that the Oedipal struggle for possession of the mother lay between the child and the mother's brother rather than the child and the father (see Malinowski 1927, 1929). More recently Keesing (1981) has raised the question again in somewhat rhetorical terms.

Is the Oedipus complex really universal in human experience? Did the hostility of father and infant son, and rivalry over the mother's sexuality, which Freud viewed as central in human psychology everywhere, take the same form and have the same importance, where – as in the Trobriand Islands – a boy's maternal uncle, and not his father, was the stern disciplinarian? (Keesing 1981, p.102)

Unfortunately Keesing provides no answers and does not attempt to sift the evidence. In marked contrast Sudhir Kakar argues that the Oedipal complex takes a very different form in an Indian setting. Quoting from the writings of Girindrashekar Bose, the founder of Indian psychoanalysis, Kakar, himself a practising psychoanalyst, maintains that from the outset psychoanalysis in India has had to adapt to cultural norms. One such adaptation is the far more *directive* role of the analyst. Kakar argues that 'the actively didactic stance of the Indian analyst, as he engages in a lively interaction with the patient, fits more with the model of the guru–disciple than the doctor–patient relationship' (Kakar 1990 p.431). It is worth noting that Cannaan (1983) writing about social work practice similarly describes a far more directive approach to clients by social workers in India than in Britain and she suggests that British social workers should eschew non-directive approaches with clients from the Indian subcontinent.

A second and more significant adaptation is due to the rich and complex variety of Hindu myths which remain vibrantly potent and active for Indian patients and which analysts ignore at their peril. Central are the myths of Devi, the great goddess, which in Kakar's view constitute the 'hegemonic narrative of Hindu culture' (ibid p.436) and represent 'the central maternal configurations of Indian culture' (ibid p.437). Through discussion of a particular patient and quoting from Bose's correspondence with Freud, Kakar argues that the central theme embodied in his male patients' fantasies is 'to maintain an idealised relationship with the maternal body' (p.438) by being or becoming a woman, a fantasy which 'is facilitated by the culture's views on sexual differentiation and the permeability of gender boundaries' (p.439). Kakar goes so far as to argue that 'when Gandhi publicly proclaims that he has mentally become a woman he is sure of a sympathetic and receptive audience' (ibid p.439). Kakar concludes that in the Indian context the rivalry between father and son 'is less that of Oedipus, the power of whose myth derives from the son's guilt over a fantasized and eventually unconscious parricide' (ibid p.442). Rather it stresses more the father's envy of what belongs to the son, including the mother – and thus the son's persecution anxiety – as a primary motivation in the father–son relationship. It is thus charged with the dread of filicide and with the son's castration, by self or the father, as a solution to the father–son competition (ibid p.443). This constitutes a major reworking of the Oedipus complex and it would appear to give different answers to different parts of Keesing's question posed earlier. It clearly indicates that the Oedipus complex does not take the same form universally but is modified by the cultural context. In the Indian examples cited by Kakar the modification is so extensive that the very term 'Oedipus complex' appears wholly inappropriate. This suggests that Freud's formulation of the father–son conflict was itself cast in terms of its own cultural context and that while the phenomenon it seeks to describe may (or may not) be universal, it appears in different forms in different places.

The Japanese psychoanalyst Takeo Doi has argued for the existence of the culture-specific concept of *amae,* which he regards as unique to Japanese society (Doi 1962, 1973, 1990). Doi argues that a characteristic of Japanese society is 'the tolerance for dependent relationships' reflected in 'the existence of a special vocabulary in Japanese to express various phases of emotional dependence' (Doi 1990 p.449). Within this vocabulary the concept of *amae* is pivotal, expressing what an infant feels toward its mother, when it wants to come close to her and is accepted by her (ibid p.450). Linguistically the word derives from a group of words indicating sweetness (see Doi 1962) and in the psychological context 'refers to the tendency of a person self-indulgently to expect and even take advantage of the help and support of individuals and groups close to him or her' (Miyake et al. 1985 p.279). Doi (1973) argues that Japanese infants experience a sense of 'perfect oneness' with their social environment up to the age of about 7 months. This is due to Japanese child-rearing practice which emphasises very close physical contact between mother and child through breast-feeding, co-bathing, sleeping together, tactile communication, carrying the child on the mother's back (see Lebra 1976, Caudill and Weinstein 1969 for extended discussion). At the age of about 7–8 months, according to Doi, the Japanese infant begins to become aware of the mother's separate existence and thereafter longs 'for a return to the state of "perfect oneness" with the mother, and also longs to return to the state of *amae*' (Miyake et al. 1985 p.280). Doi's formulation of the concept of *amae* is particularly interesting since it has informed research into the nature of attachment between Japanese infants and their mothers, which is reviewed below.

The Strange Situation Test

Studies of patterns of attachment have used Ainsworth's Strange Situation Test (Ainsworth et al. 1978), in which 'infants are observed in an unfamiliar

68

playroom, where they are given an opportunity to explore toys as well as to interact with an unfamiliar adult in the presence and in the absence of the mother' (Bretherton 1985 p.15). Particularly significant is the infant response to the mother's return. The optimum response is to approach the mother and seek physical contact if her absence has caused distress, and where it has not, to greet her and interact with her (Group B response). Some infants snubbed or avoided the mother (Group A response) while others showed a mixed response of angry, resistant behaviour with tantrums interspersed with attachment behaviour (Group C response). These patterns were described by Ainsworth following a study of the interaction between middle class white American mothers and their infants in Baltimore, and they have been replicated and refined in various studies since (see Bretherton 1985 for further discussion).

Interestingly Ainsworth's thinking about these attachment patterns was prompted by her observations of Ganda mothers and infants in 1954–5 (see Ainsworth 1967 for full discussion). In a later summary of the Ganda and Baltimore studies, Ainsworth argued that a higher proportion of Ganda infants seemed to be securely attached to their mothers and yet they registered intense separation protest more frequently than their American counterparts (Ainsworth 1977 p.146). Furthermore their response to strangers was far more marked by anxiety and fear. Ainsworth accounts for this in terms of the Ganda and Baltimore infants' very different life experiences. The former have very little experience of strangers although their contact with family, neighbours and relatives may be much greater. The American sample, by contrast, were 'taken relatively frequently to supermarkets and other places where they encountered unfamiliar people in great variety, under circumstances of proximity and often interaction and even contact' (ibid p.142). Implicit in this account is the notion that *the reasons for the Ganda children's behaviour cannot be understood without reference to their societal context or life style.* Ainsworth attributes the higher proportion of secure attachments in the Ganda sample as being due to very different child care practices. Thus the majority of Ganda infants were breast-fed whereas the Baltimore infants were largely bottle-fed. Ganda infants spent far more time with their mothers or in close proximity with them and had more physical contact with them. Because of the differences in form between the two studies direct comparisons are difficult and Ainsworth does not attempt to evaluate the degree of maternal responsiveness amongst the Ganda group. Furthermore Ainsworth does not try to apply the Strange Situation Test groupings retrospectively to the Ganda infants.

Intercultural variations in the Strange Situation Test

Grossman et al. (1985) studied a North German sample of infants and noted a preponderance of Group A responses, showing avoidant behaviour. They explain this finding in terms of cultural pressures on mothers to engage in independence training. This contrasts markedly with studies of Israeli kibbutz-reared children (Sagi et al. 1985) and of Japanese children (Miyake et al. 1985, Takahishi 1986). These studies found that resistant (Group C) responses were more numerous than would have been expected from North American studies. Miyake et al. (1985) reported that Japanese babies, who had very little experience of caregivers from outside the family, found the Strange Situation extremely stressful. Similarly Sagi et al. (1985), who observed infant interaction with mother, father and with *metapelet* (substitute caregiver), found that their infants reacted with such distress to the Strange Situation Test that 35% of the sessions had to be terminated (p.266). They also ascribe this response to the infants' unfamiliarity with strangers, recalling once again Ganda children's response to strangers. Once more the *resistant response may tell observers more about the life style of the children being tested than about the nature or strength of the attachment relationship*. This view receives further confirmation when the results from an Israeli city-based sample are considered. Sagi and Lewkowicz (1987) again found resistant (Group C) responses more common than in the Baltimore study and far more common than the avoidant (Group A) responses, but there were fewer resistant (Group C) responses amongst city-reared Israeli children compared with the Kibbutz-reared children. In other words there were significant *intracultural* differences within Israeli society, which reflected the different life experiences of children growing up in very different environments. These findings also raise questions about *the cultural bias inherent in the Strange Situation Test,* a matter raised by Takahashi (1986).

Intracultural variations in the Strange Situation Test

The significance of intracultural variations in attachment patterns has been highlighted by Van IJzendoorn and Kroonenberg (1988) who reviewed 32 studies of attachment in 8 societies. Of these studies 18 were conducted in the USA, 4 in the Netherlands, 3 in West Germany, 2 in Israel and in Japan and 1 each in Great Britain, Sweden and China. In all studies except one, secure (Group B) responses were in the majority, the exception being the Bielefeld study by Grossman et al. (1985) where avoidant (Group A) responses outnumbered secure (Group B) ones. The Chinese study by Li-Repac (1982) reported that half the sample showed Group B responses, and the other half were equally divided between Group A and Group C responses. Otherwise the European studies showed a marked preference for avoidant (Group A) over resistant (Group C) responses. The American studies were more mixed. Overall avoidant (Group A) responses were more common than resistant (Group C) ones but in five studies more resistant (Group C) responses were found than avoidant (Group A) ones, while in two others they were equally distributed. The Japanese and Israeli studies are consistent in reporting more resistant (Group C) responses than avoidant (Group A) ones.

In discussing these findings Van IJzendoorn and Kroonenberg note that some of the variations between the American studies can be related to the socioeconomic status of the samples. Thus Easterbrooks and Lamb (1979) reported 62 secure (Group B) responses, 3 avoidant (Group A responses) and only 1 resistant (Group A) response in a sample drawn from middle-class, mostly professional families. By contrast Egeland and Farber (1984) reported 188 secure (Group B) responses, 46 avoidant (Group A) responses and 48 resistant (Group C) responses in a sample which included low socioeconomic status and economically disadvantaged and maritally unstable families. They conclude that 'effects of environmental stress appear implicated as at least one factor in leading to such extreme differences' (Van IJzendoorn and Kroonenberg 1988 p.154).

The impact of environmental factors – towards an ecological approach

The emphasis on intracultural variations and the role of environmental stress factors lead us to consider their impact on parenting, on child parental interaction with children, and hence on child development. Reference was made earlier to Quinton's (1994) description of Efe multiple mothering as 'part of a different child-rearing ecology'. The notion of an ecology of child development was articulated by Bronfenbrenner (1979), and more recently African–American writers have paid greater attention to it. Such an approach looks beyond the traditional focus of much writing on child development, which concentrates on the child itself, the mother–child relationship and then on processes within the family, that is, the microsystem of the child's world. An 'ecological' approach looks more at the 'eco-system' within which the child and the family are located, thereby including the neighbourhood, the sub-culture or culture of the family, the socioeconomic status, employment status and other sociological, rather than psychological, factors which have a direct impact on the parent(s) of the child and which may therefore affect parenting.

Amongst African–American writers Ogbu (1985) has argued for 'a cultural ecology of competence among inner city blacks' and others have drawn attention to the impact of poverty on the development of black children (McAdoo and McAdoo 1985, McLoyd 1990, McLoyd and Flanagan 1990, McLoyd and Wilson 1991, Slaughter 1988). Much of this literature is reviewed by Barbarin (1993) who notes that 'a degree of consensus is building around the relationship between several contextual factors, such as family functioning and poverty and the risk of psychological symptoms' (p.387). In discussing African–American families he catalogues 'potential problems within the family or household' which include 'lack of resources to provide the basic

71

necessities of life, despair and loss of hope about ability to change the family's life situation, instability of residence, overburdened parents, lack of supervision during non-school hours, strain on extended family when parents become dysfunctional, lack of respite and other child care, (lack of) recreational activities for adult caretakers and poor health of primary caretakers' (p.387). If several of these potential problems combine then one might expect that parenting abilities are adversely affected and the 'ecosystem' surrounding the child functions less well. In such circumstances it would not be surprising for any tests of attachment behaviour to show a comparatively high proportion of Group A or Group C responses in line with Egeland's and Farber's (1984) findings.

While much of this literature has referred specifically to African–American families and communities, it applies to many poor, socially disadvantaged groups trapped within the inner cities of the western world. Minority ethnic status brings major additional problems, but those listed by Barbarin are shared with the disadvantaged poor from the majority community as well as from minorities. Ambert (1994) has noted that 'parenting and childhood become more difficult when there is high unemployment and poverty, and when the economy of a country as a whole is depressed' and she reports Halpern's (1990) finding that 'poverty and deprivation make parenting problematic because they increase obstacles' (p.535). Single parenthood is a particular example where poverty and other disadvantages can combine to make parenting particularly difficult. Duncan (1991) has argued that single mothers are disproportionately represented at or below the poverty level, and Barbarin (1993) expresses his concern that 'over half of African–American children are being raised in households designated by the census as single parent families. Yet children growing up in single-adult households have a higher risk of disorders than do children in most dual-adult structures' (p.387). For the immediate purpose of this chapter the concern must be whether poor single parents can overcome the very considerable obstacles referred to by both Halpern and Barbarin and receive sufficient support to do so, from both informal and formal networks. Without arguing for a 'culture of poverty' in the manner of Lewis (1966) one can recognise that poor parents face major challenges in meeting their children's needs which can prove difficult, even insuperable. Writing on attachment has rarely addressed this and this imbalance requires redressing.

Attachment in extreme adversity – a Brazilian example

Much of the 'ecological' writing cited above has looked at older children rather than the very young children who form the subject of much of the attachment literature (for example, Barbarin and Soler 1993, Jagers and Mock 1993). However Scheper-Hughes' (1990, 1992) accounts of 'mother love and

72

child death in north east Brazil' specifically address issues of attachment and bonding in conditions of extreme adversity, characterised by poverty, deprivation, high infant mortality rates and violence. In this setting Scheper-Hughes explores the processes and meaning of mother–infant relations. Her extended account (Scheper-Hughes 1992) can indeed be seen as a very full working out of the ecological model of child development as advocated by Bronfenbrenner (1979) and as a prime example of Ambert's (1994) dictum about the increasingly problematic nature of parenting and childhood in increasingly difficult socio-economic conditions. Scheper-Hughes' extremely rich and thought-provoking material deserves wide consideration, inevitably the focus here is on the light it throws on thinking about attachment.

Scheper-Hughes describes a world where, because of high birth rates and high infant mortality rates, mothers seem wary of attaching to their infant children and are trained by their own experience and that of the older women around them, not to express their grief at the all too frequent deaths of their offspring. This can be seen as a strategy for psychological survival against overwhelming odds, adopting a deliberate indifference towards all but the most determined survivors amongst the children born to them. Thus babies are not seen as individuals, are often not named or differentiated from each other. Child care practices minimise interaction between mother and new born child. Thus 'recently delivered mothers are cautioned by older women not to "pick up" their infants until their 40 day "*resguarda*" is over'. They 'are not held a great deal and are left alone for long periods of time, lying on their backs or their stomachs in a hammock or on their mother's beds'. Breast-feeding is rare and is discouraged within the community (Scheper-Hughes 1990 p.558). What is being fashioned here, argues Scheper-Hughes, 'is a different cultural construction of the infant and small baby. The infant is human, but decidedly less human than the older child or certainly than the adult and is understood as intrinsically *less valuable* than older children or than adults' (ibid p.558, emphasis original). She continues this theme by claiming that 'no effort is made to attribute to the infant and small baby such human characteristics as consciousness, will, intentionality, self-awareness and memory . . . The infant and baby is seen as incapable of real human suffering' (ibid p.559). Consequently 'the infant's humanness, its personhood and its claims on the mother's attention and affections grow over time, slowly, tentatively and anxiously' (p.560). In this harsh environment mothers frequently ignore sick, unattractive or 'unthriving' children and leave them to die, justifying their negligence by statements that the child 'wanted' to die, would not feed or was 'taken by God'.

Scheper-Hughes describes her experience in 1966 of rescuing a neglected, wasted two year old child, Zezinho, who was being allowed by his mother to 'pass away'. She describes in detail her struggle in feeding Zezinho and the reaction of her local helpers in the crèche who told her that she was wasting

73

her time (Schepher-Hughes 1990 pp.551–553, 1992 pp.345–353). After much effort she was able to restore him to some semblance of health and his mother agreed to take him back. On her return to the township in 1982 Scheper-Hughes met the seventeen year old Zezinho, by now his mother's favourite or *'filho eleito'*, her 'arms and legs'. Scheper-Hughes describes the relationship as close, affectionate and reciprocal. She does not discuss how that relationship emerged from such very unpropitious beginnings but its strength was revealed all too poignantly on her next visit to the township in 1987 when she learned that Zezinho had been brutally murdered in the violence that characterises that society, and his mother was plunged into deep, inconsolable mourning. The following excerpt gives a hint of the vividness of the mother's grief:

Dona Nanci, if my Ze were alive today my life would not be the one that I have now, a life of suffering. None of my other children turned out like him. Even on the day he died he left my house filled with enough groceries for a month. It was almost as if he knew he would be leaving me. I couldn't eat for two weeks after the murder, but there was all this food from his hands: yams, pimentos, and beans ... The other children of mine, they only give me grief and worry, they only know how to ask for things. Ze never forgot who his mother was, even after he found himself a woman. How many mothers can say that about a son? (Scheper-Hughes 1990 p.552)

Schepher-Hughes argues from this case example that 'it is essential to look at the mother–child relationship *over time* and to follow the life history and the enfolding drama of attachment, separation and loss that shapes the cultural expressions of maternal psychology and child-rearing practice' (1990 p.553 emphasis original). In this example we do not know how the attachment relationship was formed or what caused it to flourish but it is hard to imagine a 'worse case scenario' in terms of early mother–child bonding, and there is no evidence of substitute or compensatory care-giving in Scheper-Hughes' more detailed 1992 account. In explanatory terms, attachment theory would be hard pressed to account for the strong relationship between Zezinho as a young man and his mother, nor would it seem able to predict such an outcome from Zezinho's early life experience of severe neglect and little emotional nurturance. Perhaps this case example indicates how little we know about attachment under adverse conditions and that thankfully the resilience of the human spirit can never be overestimated. In Eliot's terms the miracle has happened, for indifference has been transformed into attachment, which it resembles 'as death resembles life' and has flowered into the 'live nettle'. The painfulness of grief indicates exactly how live the nettle was and it provokes the thought that the strength of the attachment is revealed most fully by the severity of the loss experienced when the relationship ends through death or separation.

Scheper-Hughes points out that '*both* severe selective neglect *and* strong sentiments of maternal attachment co-exist, dialectically, in this highly charged and physically threatening environment' (ibid p.553, emphasis original). We know little and need to know much more about parenting and child development in analogous environments, societies faced with major upheaval in the form of war, famine, collapse or other traumatic change. Children born and growing up in environments such as the detention centres in Hong Kong for 'economic migrants' from Vietnam must face adversities that are comparable to those in Scheper-Hughes' Brazilian township (Comberford et al. 1991). Ambert (1994) echoes the need for 'research on parenting under these and other extreme conditions'. Acknowledging the physical dangers and moral dilemmas of such an enterprise she proposes that these could be overcome by 'retrospective' research after 'normal' conditions have been reestablished or families relocated. The benefits would be, in Ambert's opinion, that 'we would learn much about human resilience, not only in extreme conditions cross-culturally, but also in extreme conditions that are likely to persist or be repeated – for these wars, famines and relocations have become a way of life, part of the culture of entire generations of parents and children, and part of the general fabric of several societies' (p.534). Lest this should sound far removed from the more prosaic realities of British social work, it must be remembered that parents and children fleeing wars, famines and forced relocations have found refuge in Britain and frequently their needs are unrecognised and unmet. Thus Ambert's question 'What are the dynamics involved in the transformation of the parental role and existential experience?' is very relevant for social workers seeking to help parents and children who have faced 'unpredictable, uncontrollable and often hopeless situations' (p.534).

Conclusions

The discussion has moved, appropriately, into considering lessons to be drawn from this diverse material for practice in contemporary British society which is multi-racial, multi-cultural and increasingly divided in terms of social disadvantage. Some have been raised during the discussion, such as Kareem's warning about the myopia of British professionals in dealing with clients from other cultures, Kakar's and Cannaan's comments on the appropriateness of an overtly directive approach with clients from South Asian communities and Fernandez's strictures about the inappropriateness of an exclusively mother/child perspective when working with groups where multiple mothering is the norm. What emerges overall, however, is not a list of 'practice points' or 'handy hints for busy practitioners' (useful though these might be). Far more important is the challenge to British social work practitioners to recognise the need for cultural relativism and cultural humility in thinking about attachment and parenting. Western patterns of attachment, and the assumptions which underscore them, are not necessarily 'best'. The questions must always be asked 'best for what?' and 'best for whom?' Once parenting and mothering are recognised as socially and culturally constructed, so that they change over time and differ in different places, then the social changes described by Ambert (1994) in much of western society may well be leading to changes in parenting. If these are not reflected in our conceptualisation of parenting and mothering then we may 'place undue hardship on parents, and more specifically on mothers' (Ambert 1994 p.538).

An ecological approach, which leads professionals to examine wider social factors and the way in which they make parenting more (or less) difficult should help to avoid that 'undue hardship' and prompt professionals to think of ways which help and support families. The challenge of this chapter is to see familiar things in a new light, never easy but always worthwhile, and in the area of attachment – essential.

References

Ainsworth, M.D.S. (1967). *Infancy in Uganda: Infant care and the growth of love*. Baltimore: John Hopkins Univerity Press.

Ainsworth, M.D.S. (1977) 'Infant development and mother-infant interaction among Ganda and American families'. In Leiderman, P. H., Tulkin, S. R. and Rosenfeld, R. (eds). *Culture and Infancy* (pp. 119–149). New York: Academic Press.

Ainsworth, M.D.S., Blehar, M. C., Waters, E., & Wall, S. (1978). *Patterns of attachment: A psychological study of the Strange Situation*. Hillsdale, N. J.: Erlbaum.

Ambert, A. M. (1994). 'An International Perspective on Parenting: Social Change and Social Constructs'. *Journal of Marriage and the Family*, Vol. 56, pp.529–543.

Barbarin, O.A. (1993). 'Emotional and Social Development of African American Children'. *Journal of Black Psychology*, Vol. 19 No. 4, pp.381–390.

Barbarin, O. A. and Soler, R.E. (1993). 'Behavioural, Emotional and Academic Adjustment in a National Probability Sample of African American Children'. *Journal of Black Psychology*, Vol. 19 No. 4, pp.423–446.

Bateson, G. and Mead, M. (1942). *Balinese Character: A photographic analysis*. New York: New York Academy of Sciences.

Bavington, J. (1980) Interview in *Skin* Television programme, London Weekend Television. First broadcast 23.11.1980.

Berger, J. and Mohr, J. (1975) *A seventh man: The story of a migrant worker in Europe*. Harmondsworth: Penguin.

Bischof, N. (1975) 'A systems approach toward the functional connections of attachment and fear'. *Child Development* Vol. 46 pp. 801–817.

Blurton-Jones, N. (1972). 'Comparative aspects of mother-child contact'. In Blurton-Jones, N. (ed): *Ethological Studies of Child Behaviour* (pp.315–328). New York: Cambridge University Press.

Bowlby, J. (1958). 'The nature of the child's tie to his mother'. *International Journal of Psychoanalysis*, Vol. 39, pp. 350–373.

Bowlby, J. (1982). *Attachment and Loss: Vol. 1. Attachment* (2nd edition). New York: Basic Books.

Brazelton, T. B. (1977). 'Implications of infant development among the Mayan Indians of Mexico'. In Leiderman, P. H., Tulkin, S. R. and Rosenfeld, A. (eds). *Culture and Infancy* (pp. 151–187). New York: Academic Press.

Bretherton, I. (1985). 'Attachment theory: Retrospect and prospect'. In Bretherton, I. and Waters, E. (eds): Growing Points of Attachment Theory and Research. *Monographs of the Society for Research in Child Development*, Serial No. 209, Vol. 50 pp. 3–35.

Bronfenbrenner, U. (1979). *The ecology of human development: Experiments by nature and design*. Cambridge MA: Harvard University Press.

Cannaan, C. (1983). 'Social work, race relations and the social work curriculum'. *New Community* Vol. 11, Nos. 1–2, pp.167–174.

Caudill, W. and Weinstein, S. (1969) 'Maternal care and infant behaviour in Japan and America'. *Psychiatry*, Vol. 32, pp.12–43.

Collins, P. H. (1992) 'Black women and motherhood'. In Thorne, B. and Yalom, M. (eds.) *Rethinking the family* (pp.215–245). Boston: North Eastern University Press.

Comberford, S. A., Armour-Hileman, V. L., and Waller, S. R. (1991). *Defenceless in Detention*. Hong Kong: Refugee Concern Hong Kong.

Dixon, S., Tronick, E., Keefer, C. and Brazelton, T. B. (1981). 'Mother–infant interaction amongst the Gusii of Kenya'. In Field, T. M., Sostek, A. M., Vietze, P. and Leiderman, P. H. (eds.) *Culture and Early Interactions* (pp.149–165). Hillsdale, N. J.: Lawrence Erlbaum.

Doi, T. (1962). Amae: 'A key concept for understanding Japanese personality structure'. In Smith, R. J. and Beardsley, R. K. (eds). *Japanese culture: its development and characteristics* (pp. 132–139). London: Methuen.

Doi, T. (1973). *The Anatomy of Dependence*. Tokyo: Kodansha.

Doi, T. (1990). 'The cultural assumptions of psychoanalysis'. In Stigler, J. W., Shweder, R. A. and Herdt, G. (eds.) *Cultural Psychology: Essays on comparative human development*. (pp. 446–453) Cambridge: Cambridge University Press.

Duncan, G. J. (1991). 'The economic environment of childhood'. In Huston, A. C. (ed.) *Children in Poverty, Child Development and Public Policy* (pp.23–50) Cambridge: Cambridge University Press.

Easterbrooks, M. A., and Lamb, M. E. (1979). 'The relationship between quality of infant–mother attachment and infant competence in initial encounters with peers'. *Child Development*, Vol. 50, pp. 380–387.

Egeland, B. and Farber, E. A. (1984). 'Infant–mother attachment. Factors related to its development and changes over time'. *Child Development*, Vol. 55, pp. 753–771.

Fernandez, E. (1991). 'The cultural basis of child-rearing'. In Ferguson, B. and Browne, E. (eds.). *Health Care and Immigrants: A guide for the helping professions* (pp.97–121) Artarmon NSW: Maclennan & Petty.

Firth, R. (1936). *We, the Tikopia*. London: Allen and Unwin.

Freud, S. (1940). 'An outline of psychoanalysis'. In Strachey, J. (eds. and trans.) *The Standard Edition of the Complete Psychological Works of Sigmund Freud* (Vol. 23, pp.137–207). London: Hogarth.

Grossman, K., Grossman, K. E., Spangler, G., Seuss, G. and Unzer, L. (1985). 'Maternal sensitivity and newborns' orientation responses as related to quality of attachment in Northern Germany'. In Bretherton, I. and Waters, E. (eds.) Growing points of attachment theory and research. *Monographs of the Society for Research in Child Development*, Serial no. 209, Vol. 50, pp.233–256.

Halpern, R. (1990). 'Poverty and early childhood parenting: Toward a framework for intervention'. *American Journal of Orthopsychiatry*, Vol. 60, pp. 6–18.

Hinde, R. A. (1982). 'Attachment: some conceptual and biological issues'. In Parkes, C. and Stevenson-Hinde, J. (eds.). *The Place of Attachment in Human Behaviour* (pp.60–76). New York: Basic.

Hinde, R. A. (1991). 'A biologist looks at anthropology'. *Man*. Vol. 26, pp.583–608.

Hunter, A. G., and Ensminger, M. E. (1992). 'Diversity and fluidity in children's living arrangements: Family transitions in an urban Afro–American community'. *Journal of Marriage and the Family*, Vol. 54, pp.418–426.

Jagers, R. J. and Mock, L. O. (1993). 'Cultural and social outcomes among inner-city African American children: An Afrographic exploration'. *Journal of Black Psychology*, Vol. 19, No. 4, pp.391–405.

Jamrosik, A. (1986). 'Cross-cultural issues in child abuse and neglect: implications for methods of intervention'. Paper given at the Sixth International Congress on Child Abuse and Neglect, Sydney, Australia, 1986.

Kakar, S. (1990). 'Stories from Indian psychoanalysis: context and text'. In Stigler, J. W., Shweder, R. A. and Herdt, G. (eds.). *Cultural Psychology: Essays on comparative human development*. Cambridge: Cambridge University Press.

Kareem, J. (1992). 'The NAFSIYAT Intercultural Therapy Centre: Ideas and experience in intercultural therapy'. In Kareem, J. and Littlewood, R. (eds.). *Intercultural Therapy: Themes, interpretations and practice*. Oxford: Blackwell Scientific Publications.

Keesing, R. M. (1981). *Cultural Anthropology: A contemporary perspective* (2nd edition). Fort Worth: Holt, Rinehart and Winston.

Konner, M. (1977). 'Infancy among the Kalahari Desert San'. In Leiderman, P. H., Tulkin, S. K. and Rosenfeld, A. (eds.) *Culture and Infancy* (pp.287–328). New York: Academic Press.

Lebra, T. S. (1976). *Japanese Patterns of Behaviour*. Honolulu: University of Hawaii Press.

LeVine, R. A. (1990). 'Infant environments in psychoanalysis: a cross-cultural view'. In Stigler, J. W., Shweder, R. A. and Herdt, G. (eds.). *Cultural Psychology: Essays on comparative human development*. Cambridge: Cambridge University Press.

Lewis, O. (1966). 'The culture of poverty'. *Scientific American*, Vol. 215, No. 4, pp.19–25.

Li-Repac, D. C. (1982). *The impact of acculturation on the child-rearing attitudes and practices of Chinese–American families: consequences for the attachment process*. Unpublished doctoral dissertation, University of California, Berkeley.

Malinowski, B. (1927). *Sex and Repression in Savage Society*. London: Routledge and Kegan Paul.

Malinowski, B. (1929). *The Sexual Life of Savages in North Western Melanesia*. London: Routledge & Kegan Paul.

McAdoo, H. P., and McAdoo, J. L. (eds.) 1985. *Black Children: Social, educational and parental environments*. Beverly Hills, CA: Sage.

McLoyd, V. (1990). 'The impact of economic hardship on Black families and children: Psychological distress, parenting and socioemotional development'. *Child Development*, Vol. 61, pp.311–346.

McLoyd, V. C., and Flanagan, C. (eds.) (1990). 'Economic stress: Effects on family life and child development'. *New Directions For Child Development*, Vol. 46. San Francisco: Jossey-Bass.

McLoyd, V. C., and Wilson, L. (1991). 'The strain of living poor: Parenting, social support and child mental health'. In Huston, A. C. (ed.) *Children in Poverty: Child development and public policy*, (pp. 105–135). Cambridge: Cambridge University Press.

Miyake, K., Chen, S. J. and Campos, J. J. (1985). 'Infant temperament, mother's mode of interaction, and attachment in Japan: An interim report'. In Bretherton, I. and Waters, E. (eds.). Growing points of attachment theory and research. *Monographs of the Society for Research in Child Development*, serial no. 209, Vol. 50, pp.276–297.

Morelli, G. A., and Tronick, E. Z. (1991). 'Parenting and child development in the Efe foragers and Lese farmers of Zaire'. In Bornstein, M. H. (ed.). *Cultural Approaches to Parenting* (pp.91–114). Hillsdale, N. J.: Lawrence Erlbaum.

Murphy, L. B. (1953). 'Roots of tolerance and tensions in Indian child development'. In Murphy, G. *In the Minds of Men: The study of human behavior and social tensions in India* (pp.46–58). New York: Basic Books.

Ogbu, J. (1985). 'A cultural ecology of competence among inner-city Blacks'. In Spencer, M., Brookings, G., and Allen, W. (eds.). *Beginnings: The social and affective development of Black children* (pp.45–66). Hillsdale, N. J.: Lawrence Erlbaum.

Quinton, D. (1994). 'Cultural and community influences'. In Rutter, M., and Hay, D. F. (eds.). *Development Through Life: A handbook for clinicians* (pp.159–184). Oxford: Blackwell Scientific Publications.

Richman, A. (1983). *Learning about Communication: Cultural influences on caretaker–infant interaction.* Unpublished doctoral thesis, Harvard Graduate School of Education, Cambridge MA.

Richman, A., LeVine, R., New, R., Howrigan, G., Welles, B., and LeVine, S. (1988). 'Cultural differences in mother–infant interaction: Evidence from a five-culture study'. In LeVine, R., Miller, P., and West, M. (eds.). Parental behaviour in diverse cultures (pp.81–96). *New Directions for Child Development*, San Francisco: Jossey-Bass.

Ritchie, J., and Ritchie, J. (1981). 'Child rearing and child abuse: The Polynesian context'. In Korbin, J. E. (ed.). *Child Abuse and Neglect: Cross-cultural perspectives*. Berkeley: University of California Press.

Sagi, A., Lamb, M. E., Lewkowicz, K. S., Shoham, R., Dvir, R., and Estes, D. (1985) 'Security of infant–mother, –father, and –*metapelet* attachments among kibbutz-reared Israeli children'. In Bretherton, I., and Waters, E. (eds.). Growing points of attachment theory and research. *Monographs of the Society for Research in Child Development*, serial no. 209, Vol. 50, pp.257–275.

Sagi, A., and Lewkowicz, K. S. (1987). 'A cross-cultural evaluation of attachment research'. In Tavecchio, L. W. C., and Van IJzendoorn, M. H. (eds.). *Attachments in Social Networks: Contributions to the Bowlby-Ainsworth attachment theory* (pp.427–459). Amsterdam: Elsevier Science.

Scheper-Hughes, N. (1990). 'Mother love and child death in northeast Brazil'. In Stigler, J. W., Shweder, R. A., and Herdt, G. (eds.). *Cultural Psychology: essays on comparative human development* (pp.542–565). Cambridge: Cambridge University Press.

Scheper-Hughes, N. (1992). *Death without Weeping: The violence of everyday life in Brazil*. Berkeley: University of California Press.

Slaughter, D. (1988). *Black Children and Poverty: A developmental perspective*. San Francisco: Jossey-Bass.

Sluckin, W., Herbert, M. and Sluckin, A. (1983). *Maternal Bonding*. Oxford: Blackwell.

Takahashi, K. (1986). 'Examining the strange situation procedure with Japanese mothers and 12-month old infants'. *Developmental Psychology*, Vol. 27, No. 2, pp. 265–270.

Tronick; E. Z., Morelli, G. A., and Winn, S. (1987). 'Multiple caretaking of Efe (pygmy) infants'. *American Anthropologist*, Vol. 89, pp. 96–106.

Van IJzendoorn, M., and Kroonenberg, P. (1988). 'Cross cultural patterns of attachment: A meta-analysis of the strange situation'. *Child Development*, Vol. 59, pp.147–156.

Wilks, T. (1990). *Transcultural Bereavement Counselling: Implications for social work*. Unpublished Masters dissertation, School of Social Work, University of East Anglia, Norwich.

5 The prevalence of childhood trauma in the lives of violent young offenders

Gwyneth Boswell

This chapter aims to examine the correlation between early experiences of abuse and loss traumata and violent offending in early to late adolescence. It will draw primarily upon the author's recent research study into the experiences and backgrounds of violent young offenders (Boswell 1995) which looked, amongst other things, at the frequency of significant loss and child abuse experiences in the lives of these young people. Other relevant material derived from contemporary socio-psychological research into the genesis of violence will also be discussed in an attempt to identify such links as may exist between loss, abuse and violence. Finally, the implications for appropri-ate intervention in this complex arena will be considered.

In the present context, trauma is defined as a morbid condition of mind produced by external violence or emotional shock. Although it is well-known that the human mind is vulnerable to trauma in a variety of forms, including disasters such as earthquake and war, I shall concentrate here on the phenomena of abuse and loss, suggesting that, as products of failed or flawed attachment, they can follow a pathway common to other traumata which, *inter alia*, can lead to violent manifestation. Violent young offenders are, here, defined as those sentenced in England and Wales under Section 53 of the Children and Young Persons Act 1933.

Section 53 of the Children and Young Persons Act 1933 provides for the sentencing of young people between the ages of ten and seventeen inclusive who have committed grave crimes and for whom no other existing sentence is deemed suitable by the courts. Subsection (1) provides that such children and young persons convicted of murder be detained during Her Majesty's pleasure, that is to say for an indeterminate period. Subsection (2) provides that such children convicted of other serious crimes, usually involving actual or intended violence, which would attract a sentence of imprisonment of fourteen years or more in the case of an adult, or for indecent assault on a woman; be detained mainly for determinate periods in excess of the existing twelve month custodial limit for that age group. Common examples of this are those sentenced for manslaughter (who may be detained for life), rape, arson and robbery.

Frequency of abuse and loss: survey methodology

The aim of the survey was, over a period of one year (mid 1993–mid 1994) to obtain and analyse hard data about the nature and frequency of child abuse and loss in the backgrounds of a statistically significant number of Section 53 offenders.

The rationale for this piece of work was derived from the findings of a small-scale study which drew on interviews with 25 of the population of Section 53 offenders, then numbering 615 (Boswell 1991). An unanticipated by-product of this survey was the discovery of hard evidence that 50% of the sample had a background of some kind of child abuse (i.e. physical, sexual, emotional, organised/ritual or combinations thereof). Staff, familiar with the signs of abuse, estimated that the true figure could be as high as 90%. The next step was to look at a much higher proportion of cases to try and establish a reliable figure for the frequency of this phenomenon. In addition, I had noted from the previous study an apparent prevalence of bereavement and other significant loss experiences, and decided to add this to the list of categories to be studied in this survey. Abuse and loss are separate phenomena and yet, at times, are not unrelated especially where abuse is seen as a 'loss of trust' experience (though abuse has not been categorised as 'loss' in this survey); both constitute traumatic events for a child. This study shows that at times the two phenomena appear independently and that at other times they co-exist.

The research method was to obtain the required data on approximately one third of the mid-1993 Section 53 population by the following means:

a) To examine a random sample of 200 centrally held files on Section 53 offenders of all ages and to note down evidence in them of child abuse and loss.

b) Where evidence in these files was partial or ambiguous to interview the offenders themselves to try and establish whether they had experienced a background of child abuse and/or loss.

A team of three researchers scrutinised the files of 78 adult prisoners, 59 young offender institution inmates, and 63 Department of Health establishment residents (200 in all). Of these, 12 were women and 48 were black, broadly reflecting their proportions in the wider Section 53 population. Ages ranged from 14 to 59. One hundred were serving Section 53[1] sentences including the 59 year old who had been recalled four times; and one hundred were serving Section 53[2] sentences including eight detained for life. In addition to standard information about age, sex, ethnic background, offence and sentence length or tariff date, the five main categories studied were those of emotional, sexual, physical, organised/ritual abuse and loss. Confirmation of these phenomena by one or more trained professionals (for example doctors, psychiatrists, psychologists, probation officers, social workers) or by the recording of case conference decisions was also noted. It is, of course, arguable that the recorded confirmation of, say, one professional, may not constitute hard evidence that the phenomenon exists. However, there has to be a baseline and this at least went beyond the recording of a *suggestion* of one of these phenomena. Where only the latter was found or where the researchers (all of whom had experience in working with offenders) discerned enough factors to raise queries about its existence, the particular offender was noted as being a person who should be interviewed if possible.

Ultimately, then, 32 interviews took place, in 22 separate establishments, with 21 adult male prisoners, eight 17–20 year olds (seven males in Young Offender Institutions [YOIs] and one female serving a sentence in an adult prison), and 3 male Department of Health establishment residents. Of these, five of the adults and three of the YOI males were black. Since respondents were being asked to give information of a very personal and sensitive nature the researchers spent a considerable length of time discussing the most appropriate device to encourage them to engage with the topic as openly as possible. It was decided to begin the interview by giving each respondent a short questionnaire with eight headings inviting them to tick any which they felt applied to them. The questionnaire took the questioning one step further than the file search by inviting respondents to make an actual link between background experiences and violent offending. For quantitative purposes, however, this data is presented alongside that gained from the files in the form of background factors rather than as a cause which is highly problematic to establish in this field.

The questionnaire contained specific headings such as sexual or physical abuse but also deliberately included the broader heading of 'Problems in childhood' which respondents might find less threatening to tick at the start but with some drawing out might identify more specifically as the interview discussion 'warmed up'. There was also an 'other reason' category. Each heading was then referred to verbally by the interviewer, whether ticked or not, to allow for second thoughts and for literacy problems. Overall, although the aim was to elicit specific categories of information it was considered important for respondents themselves to feel that they had some control over the agenda for discussion if they were then to allow the information they proffered to be pursued by the interviewer.

A potential criticism of the above method is that respondents may lie about and exaggerate the listed factors in the questionnaire in order to try and justify whatever horrific crime they had committed, and that this possibility makes the supplementary evidence-gathering method less reliable than the file search method where professional corroboration was sought. There is no way of knowing whether such deception occurred and it may be that some readers will wish to treat the findings with some caution. The impression of the researchers was, however, that if anything, the opposite was the case. Most respondents spoke hesitantly about experiences which had often been deeply painful for them and, initially at least, erred towards reticence rather than excess. Almost certainly, as other interviewers in the field of child abuse have found, there were experiences of abuse which remained denied or undisclosed by some respondents. At least half a dozen, in addition, identified significant abuse or loss experiences but were adamant that they would not wish to employ these as an excuse for their own unacceptable behaviour.

A population breakdown

A profile of the current population of Section 53 offenders is provided by Table 5.1 which shows the breakdown of numbers, age-range, sex and ethnic origin in the Child Care, Young Offender Institution and Adult Prison systems respectively. The convention surrounding allocation to institutions is that youngsters under the age of sixteen will enter the Child Care system and those over sixteen, a Young Offender Institution. Those already in the Child Care system will normally transfer to a YOI at the age of eighteen years and those still in custody at the age of twenty-one years will then transfer to an adult prison (Home Office 1987).

As at 31st October 1994, 666 Section 53 offenders were detained in the Prison system and 115 in the Child Care system making a total of 781. This represented an increase of 176 since 'Waiting for Change' last reported on the Section 53 population as at 1st February 1991 (Boswell 1991). Table 5.1 denotes the institutional, gender and ethnic breakdown of the 1994 figure and shows that whilst women continue to form a small proportion (4%) of the Section 53 population, black people (largely men) constitute just over 25% of that population.

Importantly the table also shows that 550 young people under the age of 21 (i.e. 115 in the Child Care system and 435 in YOIs) are detained under Section 53, representing approximately 9% of convicted young people in custody in that age group at the same time of year. The number detained for 'grave' crimes is therefore relatively small. It is also necessary to realise that many of these young offenders serve long sentences ranging potentially from two to fifteen years (reflected in the adult prison population figure of 231) and that the numbers currently detained probably reflect an average of about 100 per year sentenced to Section 53 disposals in the present decade.

Table 5.1
Distribution of Section 53 population as at 31.10.94

Institution	Normal age range	Total number	Total male	Total female	Total white	Total black
Child Care system						
Community Homes (open or secure accommodation)	10–18 years	101	89	12 (3 black)	82	19
Youth Treatment Centres	10–18 years	14	14	–	11	3
Sub-total		115	103	12 (3 black)	93	22
Prison system						
Young Offender Institutions	16–20 years	435	424	11 (2 black)	316	119
Adult Prisons	21+	231	223	8 (1 black)	196	35
Sub-total		666	647	19 (3 black)	512	154
Total		781	750	31 (6 black)	605	176

N.B. The word 'black' is employed in these tables to denote people classed by the Home Office Statistical Division as follows: Black (African, Caribbean, Other); South Asian (Bangladeshi, Indian, Pakistani); Chinese and Other (Chinese, Asian Other, Other).

The prevalence of abuse

It is widely acknowledged that child abuse is a complex concept which does not easily lend itself to definition. However, whilst recognising the limitations, this reservation should not defeat all attempts to research the topic. For the purposes of this survey the term 'abuse' was broken down into four categories based on inter-departmental guidelines (Home Office et al. 1991) and adapted for ease of explanation and categorisation. Thus, emotional, sexual, physical and organised/ritual abuse are each defined as follows:

Emotional: Actual or likely severe adverse effect on the emotional and behavioural development of a child or adolescent caused by persistent or severe emotional ill-treatment, rejection or neglect.

Sexual: Any form of sexual exploitation of a child or adolescent, whether involving physical contact or not, by a sexually mature person.

Physical: Any form of physical injury or harm (including bullying) to a child or adolescent brought about intentionally by someone in a position of power in relation to the child or adolescent.

Organised/ritual: Any form of pre-planned abuse which may involve magical, religious, pornographic or other predictable ceremonies or procedures, often used over time emotionally, physically or sexually to abuse children or adolescents singly or in groups.

It is recognised that neglect and ritual abuse are often seen as categories in their own right. However, because of the small numbers involved they have been subsumed under emotional and organised abuse respectively for the purposes of this study. In considering the application of these definitions it has to be acknowledged that some children may be more adversely affected by some of these acts than others, some by a single act of abuse and others by spasmodic or consistent acts of abuse over time. The areas of abuse also sometimes overlap so that, for example, emotional abuse may often accompany or follow from the other categories. The key task for the researchers was to determine, via professional corroboration or personal interview, whether those on the receiving end had suffered profound negative consequences which may have had a bearing on their later violent offending behaviour. It is almost impossible to establish direct causal links between abuse and violence although, as will be seen later, some writers have made persuasive connections. Nevertheless, much can be deduced from correlating factors and Table 5.2 shows the frequency with which these 4 categories of abuse appeared in the lives of the 200 Section 53 offenders scrutinised in this survey.

Since the aim of this study was to establish the prevalence of abuse and loss factors in the overall Section 53 population the results are, for simplicity, presented as a percentage of the total sample. It should be noted, however, that suggestions in the files of abuse and loss were confirmed in the majority of interviews, and added to in a minority. An exception was the sexual abuse category where adult prisoners particularly found this, if true, difficult to discuss or disclose. Particular findings related to age, sex and ethnic background will be mentioned in the ensuing sections covering each form of abuse separately.

Table 5.2
Emotional, sexual, physical and organised/ritual abuse

Emotional abuse:	Experienced by 28.5% of the sample
Sexual abuse:	Experienced by 29% of the sample
Physical abuse:	Experienced by 40% of the sample
Organised/ritual abuse:	Experienced by 1.5% of the sample
Combinations of 2 or more of the above forms of abuse (most often physical and emotional):	Experienced by 27% of the sample

Key finding: 72% of the total sample had experienced emotional, sexual, physical or organised/ritual abuse, or combinations thereof.

Table 5.2's total figures may, on the face of it, seem high compared, for example, with the approximate 0.05% of children per year whose names have been placed on child protection registers during the first half of the 1990s (Department of Health, 1992, 1995). However, such comparisons are, on the whole, invidious since they do not match 'like with like'. It is, thus, difficult to know precisely how the figures of abuse for Section 53 offenders compare with those for the population generally. Rather, it is judged more useful to look at the present findings in relation to the notion of 'significant harm' which results when children do not recover from abusive experiences (Bentovim 1991). It seems likely that many in the current sample would fall into this category, a matter which will be of no surprise to professionals and residential carers/custodians of Section 53 offenders. Indeed, according to their observations when interviewed for the 1991 study, their only surprise will be that the figures are not as high as 90%. For this reason it should be stressed that suggestions recorded in the files *without* professional corroboration were not included in Table 5.2 unless there was interview evidence; in some instances interviews were impossible for practical reasons. A typical example is of a young woman convicted of murder who exhibited 'disturbed behaviour from an early age' and was described by her doctor at the age of nine as 'a very distressed child needing an urgent child psychiatry referral' following a urinary tract infection and an inability to use her right leg. She became unable to walk for eleven weeks but a later report described the condition as 'a functional paralysis' for which 'no organic cause could be found'. Surrounding this situation was domestic violence and disruption at home. The existence of this combination of factors would have raised the antennae of many of those accustomed to working with abused children, but the records contain no evidence of any formal abuse investigation or even of any probing questioning. For practical reasons an interview was not possible and, in itself, would have been no guarantee of an abuse disclosure.

The prevalence of loss

As explained earlier, the term 'loss' here has been used to look at the prevalence of bereavement and other significant loss experiences (see Table 5.3). The notion of loss derives from Bowlby's work on maternal deprivation (1951) and his own and Rutter's later adaptations of this thesis centering around attachment and loss (Bowlby 1969, 1973, 1980, Rutter 1972). The emergent theory is that children who experience the permanent or semi-permanent loss of a significant figure to whom they are emotionally attached may suffer serious emotional disturbance as a result. Such disturbance is thought to be more likely when, as in many of the present cases, the children have not been effectively helped to understand and resolve their loss experiences. Although the effects may appear similar to those of emotional abuse they cannot be classed in the same category since the infliction of loss is rarely an act which is consciously directed towards the child. It is, nevertheless, an experience which, in common with acts of abuse, constitutes a major source of childhood trauma which, depending on how it is handled, may later contribute to disordered behaviour, including aggression and violence.

Table 5.3
Experiences of loss

Type of loss	Parent	Grand-parent	Other relative	Other carer	Friend
Death of someone important	10%	6.5%	2.5%	1%	1%
Loss of contact with someone important	39.5%	1%	1.5%	–	1%
Total experiencing loss	49.5%	7.5%	4%	1%	2%

Key finding: 57% had experienced significant loss via bereavement or cessation of contact and in some cases both.

89

Table 5.3 shows that 57% of the violent young offenders in this sample had experienced significant loss of some kind. Again, it should be stressed that these were loss experiences deemed by professionals or the offenders themselves to have had a distinct impact upon them and their subsequent behaviour. An example of a case omitted from the 'Loss' category is a man of twenty-four years, reported to have lived in institutions almost continuously since the age of seven and a half years and who must, presumably, have had some separation experience from his immediate family. However, because little is chronicled on his file it was not possible to discern what the professional assessment of the significance of his removal to care at an early age had been. If such cases had been included the figure would have been considerably higher.

Overall key finding

In only eighteen out of 200 cases studied were there no recorded or personally reported evidences of abuse and/or loss. In other words, the total number of Section 53 offenders who had experienced one or both phenomena was 91%.

The total number who had experienced both abuse and loss was 35% suggesting that the presence of a double childhood trauma may be a potent factor in the backgrounds of violent offenders.

The following sections will offer a wider perspective upon the findings of loss and of the four abuse types. Each section will include a Section 53 offender profile selected to illustrate the kinds of processes that an experience of abuse or loss can set in motion which may ultimately lead to a violent offence by a child or young person.

Emotional abuse

Table 5.2 shows that 28.5% of the sample had experienced emotional abuse. The most common forms were via parental/family neglect, ill-treatment or rejection. Sometimes a combination of these factors applied. Neglect could be physical or emotional. For example a young man whose father had deserted the family home was left to bring up his eight siblings as best he could whilst his mother stayed in bed most of the day suffering from depression. Another particularly bright young man was physically well looked after but completely lacked emotional affection and attention from his parents who resented his intellect and favoured his (more troublesome) older brother. Ill-treatment most often involved children witnessing violent scenes between their parents or between their parents and siblings, accompanied by actual or perceived physical threats to themselves. (Pynoos & Eth [1985] have shown that many such children suffer from post-traumatic stress syndrome). Alcohol abuse was often a feature of such scenes and a small number of the sample had witnessed the sexual abuse of their mothers or sisters mainly by fathers or stepfathers. Even when they themselves were not victims, these young people were often seriously traumatised by what they had seen, and carried guilt feelings about their own inability to intervene. Other forms of ill-treatment included parental 'use' of children in particular roles such as servant, scavenger or spy. Rejection was also a common experience. Sometimes it was persistent, the child desperately trying to do all he or she could to please the parent who would consistently withhold approval and affection, frequently offering derision in its place. In other cases, rejection constituted a single but far-reaching experience like that in the life of a young man of mixed race, shunned at birth by his mother and placed in care because she thought him 'ugly and covered in black hair'. Throughout his life he had carried with him the knowledge of this rejection.

Profile

Michael, now aged twenty-eight years, was sentenced to be detained during Her Majesty's pleasure (Section 53[1]) for the murder of an elderly woman when he was sixteen. He makes links between the anger which led him to commit this offence and the unresolved anger of his childhood. From an early age he was bullied and assaulted by his elder half-brothers and became the family scapegoat. He did not have a bed of his own to sleep in until he was seven. Later his father left home and his mother had to go out to work all day.

> I tried to feed myself but I didn't really know how to. If I managed to make something, my half-brothers would mock it and then eat it up so I was left with nothing. I was often hungry. I usually only had one meal a day. I loved my mum. She was a big woman who packed a hefty punch.

Michael attracted his mother's chastisement by misbehaving to gain her attention. He got into trouble at school, stealing, fighting and truanting. He felt that no-one ever understood how distressed he was feeling and this was why his anger came out at inappropriate times. Currently he is attending an anger control group programme in the prison and is learning to channel his feelings in a more acceptable and non-damaging manner.

Sexual abuse

Table 5.2 shows that sexual abuse was experienced by 29% of the sample. This is unusual for a predominantly male population but compares broadly with Shepherd's study of convicted male juvenile prisoners, 32% of whom reported experiences of sexual abuse (Shepherd 1993). Both these findings suggest that more investigations need to be carried out in the area of sexual abuse experienced by male offenders of all ages. Sexual abuse amongst the present sample ranged from incidents of indecent exposure to regular subjection to rape, buggery and other forms of sexual assault with a predominance at the more serious end of the range. In all cases those subjected to such abuse were reported to have been notably affected by it. The common pattern in about 80% of cases was abuse in the home by a stepfather, uncle, or male family friend when the offender was under ten years. In a third of these cases the offender had gone on to sexually abuse a younger child in turn (often a sibling or half-sibling). Another recurring theme was abuse which took place outside the home, usually involving children over the age of ten and one or more homosexual adults. (It was not normally clear that this constituted 'organised' abuse but as more comes to be known about this activity it seems possible that some of these cases would fall into that category). 3% of this sexually abused group had experienced abuse in children's homes. Abuse at the hands of men was also the experience of all the women (60% of the female sample) in the sexual abuse category. Whilst adult women were very occasionally mentioned as co-abusers it was clear that most of the sexual abuse on this predominantly male group had been perpetrated by adult males.

Profile

Anthony, now aged sixteen, was sentenced to three and a half years under Section 53[2] for an offence of rape when he was fourteen.

His parents had separated when he was three. First he went to live with his father, but later when his mother remarried he moved in with her and her new husband whom he came to dislike. To his distress his natural father ceased to have contact with him for the next eight years. When Anthony was nine, his step-father was sentenced to four years' imprisonment for offences of indecency and sexual abuse towards Anthony and two siblings.

When Anthony was thirteen his natural father resumed contact with him but died shortly afterwards. Subsequently, Anthony was found to have subjected a younger half-brother to sexual abuse and was convicted also for a separate act of rape. It is possible, but by no means definite, that he will receive the length or type of help he needs during this sentence to help him come to terms with the events of his childhood and to reduce the risk which he, in turn, now poses to society.

Physical abuse

Table 5.2 shows that 40% of the sample had experienced physical abuse in earlier life. Clearly this is the highest figure in the four abuse categories and probably reflects the fact that it is the easiest category to recognise and the most socially acceptable form of abuse to admit to having experienced. Physical abuse, in this sample, included beatings, kickings and a variety of other forms of physical harm or torture. Almost all the reported incidents formed part of a regular pattern rather than a one-off act. One of the few exceptions to this was a young man who was humiliated by a teacher who dragged him from the back to the front of a bus by the hair on a school trip. It is conceivable that this interacted with other traumatic events in his life at the time to affect him deeply. Reported forms of physical abuse which were repeated, or regular, included 'military-style' disciplinings with leather belts, whips, sticks and other implements, and consistent bullying by older brothers or older/bigger schoolchildren. The majority of beatings were administered by males – fathers, step-fathers, elder brothers – though a small number were also carried out by mothers. Some victims clearly became the family scapegoats and were singled out for this treatment. For others it was part of a wider domestic scenario where mothers and siblings were also physically abused by the dominant male in the household. Significantly, as was also the case with those who had experienced sexual abuse, some of the victims of physical abuse were reported to have continuing flashbacks or recurrent dreams of these childhood events. Both categories contained accounts of young people who had attempted self-harm or suicide on one or more occasions.

Profile

Jeff, now aged thirty-one years, was sentenced to be detained during Her Majesty's pleasure (Section 53[1]) for the murder of his homosexual partner (aged thirty-eight) when he was seventeen. He makes links with this behaviour and his earlier childhood experiences.

Jeff describes a happy family life up to the age of eight when his father died suddenly on a family holiday abroad. The whole family was distraught. The next significant event Jeff recalls is his and his older brother's arrival home from school one day to find a wedding reception taking place in the family home. His mother had married a neighbour without explaining this to them beforehand nor discussing it with them afterwards. On the wedding night, the boys heard their new stepfather beating up their mother. This violence continued and then extended to the boys in the form of 'punishments'. Jeff's stepfather would usually get drunk prior to committing these assaults and, ultimately, abandoned the family leaving them in dire financial straits.

At the age of thirteen, Jeff went out to seek sources of money for the family. He was sexually solicited in a pub and offered money for sexual favours and photographs, leading to a homosexual relationship during which his partner introduced the possibility of revealing their relationship to Jeff's family. Jeff's fear of his family's reaction caused him to murder this man. He now feels that there is a chain of events linking his childhood trauma to his taking of someone else's life. Whilst in prison he has participated in psychodrama which he

93

considers has helped to rid him of some of the anger and grief surrounding his father's death and the events that followed it.

Organised/ritual abuse

This kind of abuse appears as a comparative rarity (1.5%) in this sample, as depicted in Table 5.2. On the face of it this confirms wider findings that organised abuse is rare and ritual abuse practically non-existent (La Fontaine & Sybil 1994), though the terms are generally agreed to be misleading. It is possible, however, that, as with sexual abuse ten or even five years ago, professionals dealing with these cases were not alert to the signs or asking the right questions. Certainly there were indications in more than the three identified cases that a minority of sexually abused children might have been the victims of more than a single abuser, and some involved in 'rings' of one kind or another, but corroboration appeared not to have been sought in these cases. Of the three cases identified in this sample all had been the victims of pre-planned sexual and/or emotional abuse over considerable lengths of time from the ages of ten or under. Two cases also contained reference to 'witchcraft' and the third to 'satanism' (both undefined in records) two of them within the offenders' own families. Two had also become homosexual as a consequence, they thought, of being buggered by an adult male, when aged ten and eleven years respectively. This progression confirms limited research findings of an association between boy child sexual abuse and exploitation by adult males and later homosexuality in the victim (Finkelhor 1984; Rogers and Terry 1984).

Profile

Matthew, now aged nineteen years, was sentenced to be detained during Her Majesty's pleasure (Section 53[1]) for the violent killing of a fellow pupil from his school who had threatened to expose the fact that he and Matthew, both aged fourteen and fifteen respectively, had become drawn into an adult homosexual ring. Hitherto he and the victim had posed for pornographic photographs for a group of men who have remained in touch with Matthew. Matthew himself, described in reports as a 'Satanist', has no previous criminal record but in a comment reminiscent of the media portrayal of James Bulger's killers, is described by one criminal justice official as 'a very nasty piece of work who seems innately evil.'

Matthew's earlier life was characterised by an endless series of family house moves which were never explained to him. He was never able to settle at school because of being constantly uprooted. His parents were undemonstrative and he never experienced affection or closeness from them. This lack of showing of feelings caused him in turn to bottle things up and from time to time his anger would erupt as it did on the day of his offence. Matthew is now involving himself in higher education and hoping to come to a better understanding of the significant events in his life as a result.

Loss

Table 5.3 shows that 57% of the sample had undergone significant loss experiences which, for the most part, they had not been effectively helped to work through and come to terms with. These experiences had left them with sometimes deeply buried feelings of unresolved grief or anger, which showed themselves in disruptive or aggressive behaviour, ultimately it might be argued, culminating in an act of serious violence or murder. Such loss could take many forms in addition to the more obvious one of bereavement. A number of black Section 53 offenders, for example, had spent the earlier part of their childhood in other countries and had come to the UK at pre-pubescence or early adolescence, leaving behind significant members of extended families, school friends and the only culture they had ever known. Some had never recovered from this process which had often been compounded by difficulty in integrating into a new culture, learning a new language and painful experiences of racism. The mother of one young man, whose parents had brought him to the UK at the age of eight years, had herself experienced these traumas and soon after arrival returned to her native country for a 'holiday'. She never returned and, at the age of nineteen, now in a Young Offender Institution, her son has not seen her since.

Another type of loss was experienced by a young woman sentenced to be detained during Her Majesty's pleasure following the murder of an elderly woman whilst she was high on drugs. Earlier in her life her father had left home and married her mother's best friend who had later committed suicide. Bewildered and angered by this chain of events, the young woman turned for comfort to drugs and sexual relationships at the age of thirteen. At the ages of fourteen and fifteen she experienced two miscarriages and felt these losses deeply. She was sure that if one or both babies had survived she would have assumed a different lifestyle to the one that led her into the offence.

Other loss experiences included removal into care (whether voluntary or compulsory), a loved sibling leaving home and not re-appearing, and most commonly, parental divorce and separation. The loss of grandparents (usually through death) who had played a key role in the person's upbringing, often in lieu of parents, was keenly stressed by a number of those in this category who were interviewed.

Profile

Robert, now aged thirty-two, was sentenced to Section 53[2] Life, fifteen years ago for offences of grievous bodily harm and attempted rape. His background

contains almost every kind of abuse but the experience which is most significant to him is that of the loss of his father who had left home when Robert was
three, for reasons which Robert did not understand; and they did not renew
contact until relatively recently during Robert's prison sentence. The day his
father left, his mother beat Robert, and such beatings continued several times
a week, until he was taken into care at the age of ten years. He has very little
memory of his life between the ages of five and seven years. His elder sister,
however, tells him that he and she were both severely sexually abused by one
of their mother's lovers during that period, and also that on one occasion
Robert was nearly strangled. Robert himself has no memory of this incident
but does know that he has panic attacks and on some occasions blackouts if
ever anyone touches his neck. He also has nightmares about being strangled.
One of his worst memories is of his mother locking him in the cellar of the
house they lived in for two hours. The cellar contained rats and he recounts an
experience of sheer terror as he tried to avoid them in the darkness.

Finally, at the age of ten, Robert was taken into care but again found
himself being consistently physically, sexually and emotionally abused. At
the age of fourteen he made the first of three unsuccessful suicide attempts.
Long-serving staff at the Children's Home he was in have recently been
convicted of abuse by the Courts, though social workers at the time did not
treat his allegations seriously. At the age of fifteen Robert returned to his
family home. He found work and spent most evenings out drinking so that he
did not have to come into close contact with his family, particularly his mother
and new stepfather, whom he strongly disliked. By this time Robert was
seriously disturbed and depressed and in a state of mind which he, his probation officer, and one of his doctors all later considered had led to his commission of a violent offence. The doctor judged that the offence was a specific
acting out of aggression against his mother. Robert himself has now made a
deliberate decision to cease contact with her. However, his renewal of contact
with his father has finally helped him to understand the reasons why his father
left, an act which devastated Robert for years and removed from him the
protection of an adult he trusted. During his fifteen years of incarceration
there has been little sign of Robert receiving professional help to try and
understand his violent behaviour and how he can avoid it in future. Instead he
has turned to religion and believes that this has expiated his feelings of anger.
A final ironic ingredient is that his newfound father is now dying of cancer.

Intervention implications

To recap, the study showed that 72% of Section 53 offenders had experienced
one or more types of abuse, and that 57% had experienced significant loss via
bereavement or cessation of contact or both. In total, 91% of the sample had
experienced one or both phenomena; 35% of the sample had experienced

both, suggesting that the presence of a double childhood trauma may be a potent factor in the backgrounds of these young violent offenders. There seems little doubt that child abuse and childhood experience of loss, when no effective opportunity is provided for the child to make sense of these experiences, constitutes unresolved trauma which is likely to manifest itself in some way at a later date. The study fleshed out this progression with case examples of children who are beaten, buggered, locked in dark cellars, tortured and humiliated. As other literature confirms, many become depressed, disturbed, violent or all three (Briere 1988; Jehu 1989).

Whilst other studies have forged modest links between early traumatic experiences and later violent/abusive behaviour (Wolfe 1987; Rutter 1989; Dodge et al. 1990; Shepherd 1993) it has nevertheless proved methodologically problematic to establish cause. Widom, for example, in two articles reviewing the empirical evidence that 'violence begets violence' shows that childhood abuse or neglect increases the risk of later violent criminal behaviour but that many other variables will intervene to determine alternative manifestations such as withdrawal or self-destructive behaviour (Widom 1989a, 1989b). Additionally, it seems likely that other mediating variables, sometimes known as 'protective factors', such as biological predispositions, environmental factors, a new and significant attachment figure, may also mitigate against earlier traumatic experiences in some cases (Garmezy 1981). Accurate assessment of the influence of these factors can only be reached by means of careful longitudinal studies such as those carried out by Farrington and West in tandem with an appropriately selected control group (Farrington 1995).

Therefore, what can most usefully be said about the findings from this study of Section 53 offenders is that they show retrospectively two sets of characteristics one or more of which is likely to be present in young people who commit violent criminal offences. If many Section 53 offenders are, as the study suggests, suffering from unresolved traumata, then it would be worth focusing work with them on its resolution. The growing body of work on post-traumatic stress disorder (Pynoos and Eth 1985; Pynoos et al. 1987; Scott and Stradling 1992) confirms that children suffer the after-effects of traumatic stress in a similar way to adults. The set of criteria commonly used to establish whether an individual is suffering from post-traumatic stress disorder (American Psychiatric Association 1987) has been linked with a set of early maladaptive schema (Young 1990) to produce a continuum between major childhood trauma and psychological morbidity in later life. Of note in relation to the present study are those maladaptive schema which include subjugation, vulnerability to harm, emotional deprivation, abandonment and loss. It was a matter of some surprise to the researchers in this study that there was little evidence from case file or interview of offenders with these traumatic backgrounds having been asked about them by professionals. This phenomenon was also found in relation to the Cleveland sexual abuse crisis

(Campbell 1988) and in a critique of issues and findings about children as victims and survivors (Yule 1993).

It is difficult to see what could be lost by professionals adopting this process of 'asking the right questions' as Johnson has successfully done in his work with violent adult prisoners (Johnson 1993) and, where appropriate, adopting post-traumatic stress counselling methods (described in Scott and Stradling 1992) to help these young people make sense of their failed or damaged attachments in relation to their later behaviour. If resolution is brought about, then prevention may well have a better chance.

References

American Psychiatric Association (1987) *Diagnostic and Statistical Manual (DSM-111-R)*, 3rd edition (revised). Washington D.C: American Psychiatric Association.

Bentovim, A. (1991) 'Significant harm in context in Adcock', M., White, R. & Hollows, A. (Eds) *Significant Harm: its management and outcome.* Croydon: Significant Publications.

Boswell, G.R. (1991), *Waiting for change: an exploration of the experiences and needs of Section 53 offenders.* London: The Prince's Trust.

Boswell, G.R. (1995), *Violent Victims: the prevalence of abuse and loss in the lives of Section 53 offenders.* London: The Prince's Trust.

Bowlby, J. (1969, 1973, 1980) *Attachment and Loss*, Vols. 1, 2 & 3. London: Hogarth Press.

Briere, J. (1988) 'The long-term clinical correlates of childhood sexual victimization'. In Prentky, R. A. and Quinsey, V. L. (Eds.) *Human Sexual Aggression: Current Perspectives.* New York: New York Academy of Sciences.

Campbell, B. (1988) *Unofficial Secrets: Child sexual Abuse: The Cleveland Case.* London: Virago.

Department of Health (1992) *Survey of children and young persons on child protection registers, year ending 31st March 1991 England.* London: H.M.S.O.

Department of Health (1995) *Survey of children and young persons on child protection registers year ending 31st March 1994 England.* London: H.M.S.O.

Dodge, K. A. et al. (1990) 'Mechanisms in the Cycle of Violence', *Science*, **250**: 1678–1681.

Farrington, D. P. (1995) 'The development of offending and antisocial behaviour from childhood: key findings from the Cambridge Study in Delinquent Development', *Journal of Child Psychology and Psychiatry*, 36(6): 929–64.

Finkelhor, D. (1984) *Child Sexual Abuse: New theory and research.* New York: Free Press.

Garmezy, N. (1981) 'Children under stress: Perspectives on antecedents and correlates of vulnerability and resistence to psychopathology'. In Rabin, A. I.. Arnoff, J., Barclay, A. M. and Zucker, R. A. (Eds) *Further Explorations in Personality*. New York: Wiley.

Home Office (1987), 'Section 53(2) – Placement of Offenders', *Circular Instruction* **31/87**, P4 Division.

Home Office, Department of Health, Department of Education and Science, Welsh Office (1991), *Working Together under the Children Act 1989. A guide to arrangements for inter-agency co-operation for the protection of children from abuse*. London: H.M.S.O.

Jehu, D. (1989) 'Long term correlates of child sexual abuse'. In Ouston, J. (Series Ed.) *The Consequences of Child Sexual Abuse*. Association for Child Psychology and Psychiatry, Occasional Papers No.3.

Johnson, R. (1993) *Intensive Work with Disordered Personalities* 1991–1993, Unpublished report to the Reed Committee, January.

La Fontaine, J. S. and Sybil, J. (1994) *The Extent and Nature of Organised Ritual Abuse*. London: Department of Health.

Pynoos, R.S. and Eth, S. (1985) 'Children traumatized by witnessing acts of personal violence: homicide, rape or suicide behaviour' in Eth, S. and Pynoos, R. S. (Eds) *Post-traumatic Disorder in Children*. Washington D.C: American Psychiatric Association.

Pynoos, R. S. et al. (1987) 'Life threat and post-traumatic stress in school-age children', *Archives of General Psychiatry*, **44**: 1057–63.

Rogers, C.M. and Terry, T. (1984). 'Clinical intervention with boy victims of sexual abuse'. In Stuart, I. R. and Greer, J. G. (Eds). *Victims of Sexual Aggression: Treatment of children, women and men*. New York: Van Nostrand Reinbold.

Rutter, M. (1972) *Maternal Deprivation Re-assssed*. Harmondsworth: Penguin.

Rutter, M. (1989) 'Intergenerational continuities and discontinuities in serious parenting difficulties', in Ciccheti, D. and Carlson, V. (Eds) *Child Maltreatment Theory and Research on the Causes and Consequences of Child Abuse and Neglect*. New York: Cambridge University Press.

Scott, M. J. and Stradling, S. G. (1992) *Counselling for Post-Traumatic Stress Disorder*. London: Newbury Park: New Delhi: Sage Counselling in Practice Series.

Shepherd, S. (1993) *Prevalence of Sexual Abuse amongst Juvenile Prisoners*. Report to Home Office.

Widom, C. S. (1989a) 'The Cycle of Violence', *Science*, **244**: 160–166

Widom, C. S. (1989b) 'Does violence beget violence? A critical examination of the literature', *Psychological Bulletin*, **106**: 3–28.

Wolfe, D. A. (1987) *Child Abuse: implications for child development and psychopathology*. New York: Sage.

Young, J. E. (1990) *Cognitive Therapy for Personality Disorders: A Schema-focused Approach*. Sarasota, F. L: Professional Resource Exchange.

Yule, W. (1993) 'Children as Victims and Survivors', in Taylor, P. J. (Ed), *Violence in Society*. Royal College of Physicians of London.

6 Maintaining relationships between parents and children who are living apart

Diana Hinings

Under favourable circumstances children are cared for by their parents throughout childhood. The relationship between parent and child is mutually satisfying and one to which the adult is unstintingly committed. Separations, when these occur, are carefully managed with the child's age and ability to cope taken into account. These fortunate children have other adults available to them, relatives and friends who are there should need arise and who can both supplement the parent's efforts and provide a safety net in the event of illness or other adversity. This is what Selma Fraiberg (1977) calls Every Child's Birthright.

For a significant minority of children, this continuity of parenting is either never established or is interrupted, sometimes by unpredictable tragic events, but more often because of parental divorce or family breakdown which results in a child going into local authority care. In these situations, one or both of the parents become 'non-residential'. The parent and child no longer share a household and the role of parent, stripped of day-to-day child rearing, becomes unclear and frequently problematic. There are no well-defined characteristics of non-residential parenting. Apart from the obligation to maintain financial support, and in the absence of a social prescription those involved have to work out a solution as best they can. So far there has been little attention paid to the way non-residential parents carry out their role and similarly little effort devoted to establishing policies or practice which could facilitate and support these relationships. The perception of parents who live apart from their children (with the exception of those whose children are in boarding school) is essentially negative. There is an assumption of failed relationships in the past and a presumption of an all too ready willingness to give up parental responsibility.

Children in local authority care and children of divorced parents are rarely considered in the same category and until the English Children Act 1989, were catered for by separate legislation. The important characteristic that both groups share, is the vulnerability to loss of a relationship with a parent. For the 'in care' children the losses are likely to be multiple – siblings, friends and a familiar neighbourhood as well as one or both parents. The study by Millham et al. (1986) of children in care reported the ease with which those who remained in care for two years lost touch with their parents. The early evidence from American research (Furstenberg et al. 1983) suggested that within two years of the marital separation the non-residential parent, nearly always the father, had given up visiting. Mitchell's study (1985) in this country found that five years after divorce 40% of children rarely or never saw their fathers. This level of withdrawal from fathering has not been replicated in subsequent American studies (Seltzer 1991) and the growth in this country of pressure groups such as Families Need Fathers indicated that the picture is more complicated than a straightforward wish on the part of non-residential fathers to give up on their children.

The importance of contact

Most of the literature concerning contact between parents and children who live apart refers to children in foster care or children's homes rather than children of divorced parents. However the evidence from research suggests that the child benefits from a continuing relationship with an absent parent whatever the reason for the separation. As long ago as 1970 Victor George wrote that children in care tended to feel 'rejected, disloyal or view parents unrealistically' in the absence of contact. Rosamund Thorpe (1974) reported that children who saw their parents and could talk to them about their past were happier in placement than those who had no similar opportunity. Fanshell's (1982) study of children in care in the United States arrived at a similar conclusion and the author referred to the 'profound insult' experienced by a child whose parents seem to care so little for him that they did not visit to see how he was faring.

Wallerstein and Kelly (1980) and Wallerstein and Johnston (1990) studied the process of adjustment in families following divorce. Their research revealed a variety of potential outcomes for the children depending on their age at the time of the separation, the quality of their relationship with each parent and the child's understanding of the divorce itself. They concluded that the relationship between a child and the parent who lived separately, usually the father, remained important even when a child had a good relationship with a step-parent. It seems that a substitute parent and an original parent do not compete for the same place in a child's life.

The balance of evidence concerning contact between parents and children who live apart falls convincingly on the side of maintaining these relationships, yet in practice there is evidence that contact is often lost. The reasons why parents of children in care do not visit are well documented (Millham et al. 1986; Hess and Proch 1988). Similarly, parents who divorce have voiced

their reasons for withdrawing from the relationship with their children: a feeling that a step-parent has taken their place, that visits are a cause of distress to a child, that the practicalities are overwhelmingly difficult (either lack of money for travel or somewhere to take the child) and sometimes because the parent with whom the child normally lives denies access to the non-residential parent. All these emotional and practical pressures are understandable. What is much more puzzling is the apparently weak commitment from social workers and family court welfare officers to support contact in individual cases.

The work of Goldstein, Freud and Solnit (1973) has been very influential and their arguments extremely persuasive in relation to child care policy and planning. It also provides a theoretical legitimacy for severing relationships with separated parents. The authors state that a child's primary need is for a parent who is warmly responsive, consistent and predictable. So far this is uncontentious. However, they also maintain that if the parent is unable or unwilling to carry out the parenting role in a satisfactory manner then another adult should be sought who can do so. This substitute parent who has day-to-day care of the child earns the child's affection and becomes the psychological parent. In order to maximise the possibility of this relationship succeeding, the psychological parent must have unfettered authority in relation to the child. If the psychological parent is required to consult others on matters of parenting then the child will doubt the parent's capacity to provide protection and security. It follows from this reasoning that the day-to-day parent must decide whether a child's non-residential parent can visit or have any other kind of contact. In this scheme of things the original parent is not very significant. The child's needs are satisfied without the involvement of the original parents who may be considered to have forfeited their rights to the child.

This framework for organising parenting in cases of divorce or foster care found favour among child care social workers. It had clarity and reduced the number of people whose feelings and actions had to be taken into account. The number of children adopted from care increased as birth parents either voluntarily or compulsorily slipped out of the picture. Step-parents, again usually fathers, adopted their step-children. It seems possible that the apparent success achieved with 'classical adoption' which involved the complete severance of birth family relationships, and could be described as the nearest thing to a cure in medical terms that social work has ever achieved, might be possible for all children whose lives were affected by a breakdown in family relationships. Therapeutic techniques were developed in relation to the placement of older children whose parents were no longer a physical presence in their lives, and tools such as Life Story books have since become a standard part of a social worker's repertoire.

The case of Mrs Baker and her children provides an illustration of how easily a parent and child can lose touch and the obstacles that even a persistent

parent faces if the social worker considers contact is unnecessary or un-desirable.

Lisa was six and Adam two when Mrs Baker decided that she could no longer live with her husband. He began to drink excessively following a head injury in an off–shore accident and when he urinated on Adam as the child slept in his cot, she felt that she must act. Her plan was not particularly wise – she left the two children in the care of friends who were visited regularly by a social worker. Mrs Baker liked the idea of someone keeping an eye on Lisa and Adam and was not worried when she telephoned her friends and was told that social services had taken the children to a foster home. Mrs Baker maintains that social services always knew her address and that she was away only three weeks before she found a holiday cottage in a seaside town. She had no doubt that Lisa and Adam would be returned to her when she asked.

When Mrs Baker returned to her home town she went to social services and was assured that although a care order had been made in respect of the children, it was intended to return the children home as soon as Mrs Baker was settled. She was urged to find suitable accommodation – her husband had meanwhile abandoned the tenancy of their council house by handing in the keys. The holiday cottage was not considered suitable so Mrs Baker set about finding somewhere else. She visited the children in their foster home weekly. Mrs Baker resented the foster mother whom the children were already calling Mummy and who was telling them how big a Christmas tree they would have. She was very angry when the foster mother cut Lisa's long hair but said nothing because she thought that the children would be home soon.

Mrs Baker meanwhile met the man who was to become her partner. They moved to a town sixty miles away where they rented a two-bedroomed flat and Mrs Baker's partner found work. Mrs Baker asked to have the children home but nothing happened. She and Jim, her partner, continued to visit Lisa and Adam and they were allowed to take the children out. This state of affairs continued for more than a year and Mrs Baker decided that she would seek legal advice. Soon after Mrs Baker discovered that she was pregnant and because she was unwell, could not travel to see the children. Their foster mother considered that Adam was too young to travel with a volunteer driver and Jim was not considered a suitable person because he had no legal relationship with the children. When Mrs Baker was able to travel some six months later she was told that the children did not want to see her.

The gap between Mrs Baker and the children was now established. The foster parents moved house to another town later that year and apart from the Christmas and birthday cards which Mrs Baker sent to the children via the social worker there was no other contact for four years. Mrs Baker was very shocked when a policeman called at her house looking for Adam who had run away from his foster home. She explained that she had not seen him. Adam was found the next day but his foster parents would not have him back. Two months later Lisa stayed overnight with a school friend and she refused to

return to her foster home. She would not even go with her social worker to pick up her belongings. Since their unplanned and abrupt departure neither she nor Adam have had any contact with their foster parents, with whom they lived for eight years.

The two children now live in separate foster homes. Lisa wants her own flat and professes total confidence that she can manage perfectly well on her own. Adam is in his second placement since leaving his long term foster parents. Both children see their mother regularly. Adam would like to live with her but Mrs Baker doubts that she could manage him. Mrs Baker sums up her feelings about Lisa and Adam when she says 'they went into care as two normal kids and they've turned into two head cases'.

Mrs Baker's case can now be viewed with hindsight, a luxury not available to the social worker, and it is clear that Lisa and Adam lost more than they gained when their mother's visits stopped. Lisa recently asked her mother whether she and Adam had been abused. Mrs Baker was horrified at the question and spent time trying to prove to Lisa that their lives together before they went into care were mostly happy. Lisa said that she thought children who stayed a long time with foster parents must have cruel parents or else the parents did not want the children. Mrs Baker found it painful and frustrating to talk to her daughter and felt that Lisa had made up her mind that things had happened when it was all in her imagination. It seems that Lisa needed to make sense of her situation and she could think of no other reasons why she and Adam were in care and her mother no longer visited. Adam's distress is less pronounced but he said that he thought his mother could have fetched him home if she had really wanted him. Unfortunately now that Mrs Baker has the choice she feels she must leave her son in care.

Contact for its own sake

Although contact between parents and children who live apart has legislative support in the 1989 Children Act of England and Wales as well as accumulating research evidence which strongly suggests it is generally beneficial to a child's emotional health, it is often seen as a means to an end rather than an end in itself. For children in care it is frequently linked to a plan to restore a child to parents. Once a decision has been reached that an out of family placement should be found, the next step is to dilute the relationship between parent and child by limiting contact. The rationale is that the child will be reluctant to accept another family because of the close contact with a mother or father, and to allow this situation to continue is to deprive a child of new parents who can provide the care that their own parents have so clearly failed to do.

Contact is also seen as an opportunity for direct observation of a parent's relationship to a child. A parent who wants contact at any price may be able to forget the assessment agenda during a visit but for many parents this is a tall order. The artificiality of the meeting, the frequently unsuitable venue and the difficulty of behaving normally when being observed are all likely to make such visits an unreliable indicator of the true quality of the relationship.

Tara sees her ten month old daughter Tania twice weekly at a supervised contact centre. The routine of visits is well established and Tara and Tania enjoy each other's company. Tara says that her visits to Tania are the happiest times of her week and the centre staff joke that the contact centre is Tara's second home.

Tara knows that a decision will soon be reached about her daughter's future – Tania will either go to long term foster parents or Tara will be given a last chance to bring her up. Everyone agrees that Tara was a good mother to Tania most of the time but sometimes she would ask a friend to look after the baby 'for an hour' and then disappear for three or four days. Tara has doubts whether she has the self-discipline to look after her daughter full time and talks to the centre staff about her worries. She tells a different story to the social worker because she fears that she will lose the regular visits to Tania once it is decided that Tania will not be returned to her. Her social worker is very pleased with Tara because she attends for contact visits very conscientiously and relates warmly to her daughter.

Parents like Tara, who co-operate with social services' plans, arrive on time for visits and refrain from talking about their problems during contact meetings give a misleadingly positive impression of their capacity to care for a child full time. Ironically, parents who are more distressed by the separation from their child and are resistant to the framework of visits set in place by the social worker, may be preoccupied and overwhelmed by their feelings during contact visits and give a poor impression of their ability to look after their children.

Parents who are in conflict about arrangements for their children following divorce have assistance from a family court welfare officer. While practice varies, the aim of the court welfare officer is likely to include improving communication between the parents and reducing the level of conflict to a point where the parents can negotiate directly with each other about contact and other matters concerning the children. There is pressure to reach this point quickly because resources are finite and new families come through the system all the time. Many couples are too angry with each other to meet together with the welfare officer and the only time that they are in the same building at the same time is the occasion of contact. In these circumstances it is tempting to cash in on the opportunity of, if not a joint interview, then some discussion with both parents. Apart from the near inevitability of failure in circumstances when both parents are so resistant to contact with each other, the negative feelings which result are likely to spill over to the contact with the child. Achieving relaxed and comfortable contact between the non-residential parent and child becomes very difficult in these conditions and what is already a conflictual situation becomes further inflamed.

Achieving successful contact

Maintaining relationships and keeping in contact consumes time, money and effort. This is the case for all relationships where those concerned do not naturally meet up on a day-to-day basis. Where the separation is a consequence of divorce or family breakdown and the relationship to be maintained is one between a parent and his or her own child, there is an overlay of guilt and anger which makes keeping in contact more difficult still. If any of the adults involved in the contact, whether foster parent and birth parent or parents who have divorced, are hostile to contact taking place, then this weighs heavily against the relationship being maintained. In these circumstances the attempt to keep contact is sometimes abandoned and in others it leads to an interminable series of court hearings. Neither solution is satisfactory or brings relief even from the adult's point of view, let alone the child's.

The case of Angie and Leroy and their daughter Sonia provides an example of parents who persisted in conflict and whose lives were dominated for several years by litigation.

Angie and Leroy separated when Sonia was only a year old. Angie admitted that the marriage had been a mistake and that she agreed to marry Leroy only to escape an unhappy situation at home. Angie came to England from the West Indies as a teenager, and joined her mother and step-father. She was resented by her step-father and used as a drudge by her mother. Angie thought that her husband would go out on his own a great deal after they were married and that he would continue to be as generous with his money as he had been when he was courting her. Leroy proved to be a controlling husband who would not let Angie work outside the home and who resented her having any interests of her own.

Angie was prepared for Leroy to see his daughter regularly after their separation but every time she and Leroy met, a blazing row took place. Angie explained that her husband could not understand that he could no longer tell her what to do. Angie's main concern was to avoid Leroy and she was convinced that he wanted to see his daughter mainly because it afforded an opportunity to pressure Angie to return to him. Angie decided to change her address without telling her husband. Leroy found her some months later and when Angie refused him access to Sonia, he applied to the court and was awarded contact every two weeks. This arrangement was no more successful because Sonia, who scarcely knew her father by now, clung to her mother when Leroy moved to pick her up. This made Leroy angry and a furious quarrel between the couple followed. Angie again moved to put herself and her daughter out of Leroy's reach. This time she went further away and it took two years before she was found and once again was served with a notice to appear in court. Angie received a severe warning from the court about the consequences if she did not comply with the order and allow Leroy to see his daughter. The judge ordered that contact should take place at a contact centre.

Angie took Sonia to the centre on two occasions before deciding that she would defy the court rather than make her daughter unhappy. Angie explained that her husband behaved in the same old way, always expecting people to do what he said. Sonia became upset when her father shouted, and when Sonia cried, her father shouted all the more. Leroy went back to court and Angie expected that she would, at least, be threatened with prison. Instead the judge seemed to understand that there was a serious problem and ordered that contact should take place at a supervised centre where there were social workers on hand.

Sonia and her parents provide a good example of a family with seemingly intractable problems about contact. The occasion of contact was distressing for everyone and only Leroy's persistence kept the issue alive. If Angie and Sonia had been left to decide, they would have voted strongly against any further meetings. Everything points to yet another failure: the family has a history of contact which has gone wrong, the parents are bitterly hostile to each other, Sonia has no recollection of her family as an intact unit and the meetings which have occurred so far have revealed a father who intimidates both Sonia and her mother. How then can any change be brought about?

Supported contact

The supervised contact centre is designed to offer comfortable and homely surroundings for children and adults who are involved in difficult contact. The centre is a self-contained flat with sitting rooms, kitchen and toilet. It is carefully furnished and there are pictures, ornaments and plants in every room. The aim is to provide an environment which enhances the self esteem of those using the centre. The children, from toddlers to teenagers, have an excellent supply of toys and games. The centre staff make great effort to ensure that the rooms are attractive to children as well as adults, and there are plenty of interesting ornaments at eye level.

It is recognised that the occasion of contact is likely to be stressful and a source of considerable anxiety for all those involved. This is particularly the case before any successful meetings have taken place and contact is associated with court hearings and past hostilities. It is therefore very important that anxiety is minimized because adults and children alike, are more likely to keep control of their feelings if they feel in safe hands. There are a number of ways that this can be achieved.

First and foremost is establishing predictability. Knowing exactly what will happen helps parents and children anticipate and prepare for the contact. A centre social worker meets with the contact parent separately from the residential parent and the child before any arrangements are made. Everyone is shown round the centre and made familiar with the facilities. The social worker explains that the single purpose of the centre is to allow a child to have contact with a parent or relative. Centre staff do not provide court reports or assessments for social service departments. (Social workers and family court welfare officers may observe a contact themselves or examine records kept by the centre.) The details of the contact, which room will be used, where the other parent will wait, how long a child will remain at the centre if the contact parent does not attend, is agreed in advance. In cases where sexual abuse has been alleged a parent may, for example, be told not to adjust a child's clothing or assist with toileting.

It is taken for granted that both adults and children need practical and emotional support if contact is to be achieved. It is important that no unnecessary demands are made on either adults or children. If parents are highly antagonistic to each other they are reassured that there is no need for them to meet. They can arrive and leave at separate times. A grandmother who brings her granddaughter for contact with the child's father is so hostile to him that she speaks in a whisper in case he has any sense of her presence in the building. Few parents and relatives are as extreme in their reactions as this grandmother, but it is not uncommon for parents to say that they are willing to bring a child for contact so long as *they* do not have to have contact as well. Hostile parents who deeply resent the other parent's claim on the child usually find the act of handover extremely difficult. Again, parents can be spared this ordeal and the child in turn is spared the emotional pressure that is the unavoidable consequence of being the focus of contested contact. The centre worker acts as the bridge between the two parents and at the same time demonstrates to the child that both parents are equally respected.

The parent's view of each other, and of their situation, is left unchallenged – there is no demand to change or understand the other's point of view. After sometimes years of conflict interspersed with mediation, the recognition that, for the time being at least, their position is accepted, lessens the likelihood of hostilities being ignited and spoiling contact. At best it offers parents the possibility of lowering their defences and giving recognition that the other parent has genuine feelings for the child.

The staff at the centre are careful to be even-handed in relation to the adults involved in a contact. This is an irritation to some parents who feel very strongly that right is on their side and that a degree of partiality is appropriate. They hint that the other parent is putting on an act. Comments such as 'he won't be able to keep it up for long – he likes his drink too much' are not uncommon. Staff always respond with a neutral comment to the invitation to take sides.

Parents (or other carers) are greeted on arrival and refreshments are routinely provided. Every effort is made to remember individual preferences, for example, does she prefer coffee with or without milk. A young father who had a fearsome reputation for angry outbursts, arrived for contact saying that he had been unable to sleep the previous night because he had a bad cold. He was offered and accepted Lem-sip and said that he felt much better afterwards. There is no restriction on smoking at the centre because it is considered that some parents find smoking helps them remain calm. The staff pay friendly attention to whatever is the issue of the moment for parents and children whether or not it relates directly to the contact. It is recognised that the parent who brings a child for contact feels vulnerable and bereft while the visit is taking place and the availability of a social worker to attend to that parent is important. Most parents chose to wait in the centre during the contact although there are shops and other diversions nearby.

Role of the centre worker

The centre staff provide the framework for the contact. They take responsibility for the logistics – who goes where and when. At the same time they establish an emotional climate of neutrality and acceptance, and act as containers of anxious and angry feelings.

When a contact is in progress, a social worker is present throughout. The supervising worker is a participant in the meeting, not simply as an observer. Surprisingly, parents seem to prefer a worker who actively facilitates the contact, to one who observes from the sidelines. What might be experienced as intrusion is generally felt to be helpful. The worker sees to practical matters such as mopping up spillages but more importantly, eases communication by modelling what to say and putting feelings into words. It is often the case that a parent and young child may not have seen each other for several months while a court decides a contact issue. Such a parent may be very unsure how to approach a child, who will in turn be uncertain and fearful until a degree of familiarity between the two is established. The presence of the centre worker, who will have talked or played with the child in the presence of the other parent, gives confidence to a child that it is safe to enjoy the attention which the contact parent is wanting to offer.

The case of Mandy and Colin illustrates some of the complexities which occur when a parent seeks contact with a very young child and when the relationship between the parents scarcely exists apart from their parenting role.

Mandy and Colin had an on–off relationship for five years but never considered sharing a home. This equilibrium was upset when Mandy became pregnant. She told Colin about the baby but in the same breath said that she intended to seek an abortion. Colin said that she had no right to take this decision because he very much wanted the child and pointed out that neither of them may get another chance. Both Mandy and Colin were close to their fortieth birthday. Mandy went ahead with the pregnancy and had infrequent and quarrelsome contact with Colin. After daughter Amy was born, Mandy went home to Canada but was desperately disappointed by her mother's lukewarm reception to her and to Amy. Mandy returned to England after three months and set up home with her daughter. Mandy maintains that she never stopped Colin seeing Amy but could not cope with his threatening behaviour. Colin claims that Mandy manufactured any 'threats' but soon the police were involved and Colin was prevented by a court injunction from making contact with Mandy. Colin applied to the court for access to Amy. Mandy agreed to this, providing the contact was supervised. By this time Amy was ten months old. She was strongly attached to her mother who had been her sole carer since birth. Amy could crawl and was alert and very interested in her surroundings.

At the first contact meeting Mandy and Colin were sitting in separate rooms on opposite sides of the hall. Amy was happily exploring her mother's room and soon was sufficiently curious to venture into the hallway. The supervising worker encouraged Amy to investigate the room opposite, all the time talking to Amy about her father being in there and wanting to see her. At the same time that Amy was needing encouragement, Mandy needed the cues from the worker that she should stay put. When Amy saw her father she scuttled back to her mother's room but again curiosity won and she allowed the worker to pick her up and carry her into her father's room. Colin was primed not to approach Amy at this stage. Amy realised that she could move between the two rooms and graduated from playing peek-a-boo with her father to moving close by and passing him toys. Colin found the meeting a very emotional occasion and was lavish in his appreciation of how beautiful and intelligent his daughter was. The parents talked briefly in the corridor as Amy moved between her parents but they then retreated to their separate territory.

In contrast to Mandy and Colin where supervision was needed to assist the parents in managing their relationship with each other, Jean and Martin required supervision to reassure Jean that no harm would come to Tom, their five-year-old son. Jean had no doubt that Martin had sexually abused Tom although Martin vehemently denied the accusation. After Jean left Martin, taking Tom with her, Martin had weekly contact with his son, including overnight stays. The parents had the minimum possible contact each other. Jean explained that she felt such dislike for her ex-partner that if she could not get her sister to take Tom to meet up with his father, she would have to go, but rather than get too close to Martin, would give the child's pushchair an extra hard shove so that she could avoid the possibility of touching him. This arrangement came to an abrupt end when, according to Jean, Tom disclosed that his father had been sexually abusing him during access visits. There was no physical evidence of abuse and no basis for Martin to be prosecuted. When Martin applied for contact with his son, this was allowed four times a year providing the contact was supervised.

Contact meetings between Tom and his father are occasions of considerable excitement for Tom because Martin brings him many lavish presents. Martin greatly resents the need for supervision but takes comfort from the judge's decision to allow contact and feels that this means that Jean's accusation was seen as a cruel attempt to deprive him of his son. Jean finds contact visits very stressful because she promised Tom that he would never have to see his father again and she wishes that she could convince the judge that Martin is an abuser. The fact that Martin buys Tom any and every toy he asks for, is yet another problem. Jean is very dependent on the centre worker to 'get through' the visit. The worker reassures Jean that she has done well to help Tom cope with contact and reminds her that the visit is supervised throughout and there is no risk to Tom. Jean is able to respond to Tom when he rushes back to her with his new toys, and for him at least the contact seems relaxed and pleasurable.

Conclusion

Children and parents who live apart usually do so as a consequence of marriage or family breakdown. The last decade has seen a steady and substantial growth in the number of children affected by divorce, and an unquantifiable number more born to unmarried parents who subsequently separated. The number of children looked after or in care of a local authority has in contrast declined by a third in the same period, but still amounts to 50,000 children, most of whom live apart from both parents (D.O.H. 1994/95). The evidence from research indicates that however poorly parents fulfill their role, they have a significance and importance for the child, and maintenance of the relationship is beneficial. In spite of this clear message, child care social workers have been slow to develop practice in relation to contact.

Maintaining contact in cases where the parents (or other carers) are hostile to each other and opposed to contact is undeniably difficult, and demands skilful and surefooted practice. The insights from attachment theory underline the importance of responding to the anxiety of those involved in contentious contact and their need for support and security. Unless the parents are afforded this assistance, and discord and distress find a response, the experience of contact for the child is bound to be adversely affected. In extreme cases the child refuses contact or is so obviously distressed that contact is abandoned. This is sometimes seen as evidence that contact should never have been arranged in the first place, rather than contact poorly handled.

The loss of a relationship with a parent has well documented negative consequences in both the short and long term. Many children blame themselves if a parent leaves and the sense of loss is greater if that parent then fails to keep in touch. Bowlby (1985) reminds us that threats to abandon a child are 'a degree more frightening' than threats to withdraw love. The issue here is not the competence of a parent to care for a child in the future, or their record of parenting in the past, but the insult to the child's self esteem if the parent apparently gives up on the relationship.

References

Bowlby, J. (1975) *Attachment and Loss Vol 2. Separation: Anxiety and Anger.* Harmansworth: Penguin.

Bowlby, J. (1988) *A Secure Base: Clinical Applications of Attachment Theory* London: Routledge.

Bray, J. H. & Depner, C.E. (1993) 'Perspectives on Non-residential Parenting', in *Non-residential Parenting* eds Depner, C.E. and Bray, J.H. London: Sage.

Fanshel, D. & Shinn, E. B. 1978 *Children in Foster Care* Columbia: Columbia University Press.

Fox, Harding L. (1991) *Perspectives in Child Care Policy* London: Langman.

Fraiberg, S. (1977) *Every Child's Birthright: In Defence of Mothering* New York: Basic Books.

Furstenburg, F.F., Jr. Nord, C. W. Peterson, J.L. & Zill, N. (1983) 'The Life Course of Children of Divorce: Marital disruption and parental contact' *American Sociological Review* 48 (3) 656–668.

Department of Health (1995) *Partners in Caring. Fourth Annual Report of the Chief Inspector Social Services Inspectorate* 1994/95 London HMSO.

Goldstein, J., Freud, A. & Solnit, A. J. (1973) *Beyond The Best Interests of the Child* London: Collier Macmillan.

Hess, P.M. & Proch, K.O. 1988 *Contact: Managing Visits to Children Looked After Away From Home* London: BAAF.

Millham, S., Bullock, R., Hosie, K. & Haak, M. (1986) *Lost In Care: The Problem of Maintaining Links Between Children In Care and Their Families* Aldershot: Gower.

Mitchel, A. (1985) *Children in the Middle: Living Through Divorce* London: Tavistock.

Neil, Elsbeth (1995) *Children After Divorce, A Child Focused Social Work Response* Social Work Monographs: University of East Anglia: Norwich.

Seltzer, J.A. Schaefler, N.C. & Charing, H. (1989) 'Family ties after divorce: The relationship between visiting and paying child support' *Journal of Marriage and the Family*, 51 (4) 1013–1031.

Simpson, B. (1994) 'Access and Child Contact Centres in England and Wales: an ethnographic perspective' *Children and Society* 8:1 pp.42–54.

Thorpe, R. (1974) *The Social and Psychological Situation of the Long-Term Foster Child with Regard to his Natural Parents* PhD Thesis: University of Nottingham.

Trasler, G. (1960) *In Place of Parents* London: Routledge and Kegan Paul.

Wallerstein, J. S. & Johnston, J. R. (1990) 'Children of Divorce: Recent findings regarding long term effects & recent studies of joint & sole custody' *Paediatrics Review* 11 (7) pp.197–204.

Wallerstein, J.S. & Kelly, J.B. (1980) *Surviving The Break-up – How Parents and Children cope with Divorce* London: Grant McIntyre.

7   Loss in childhood and paternal imprisonment

Peter Wedge

This chapter will focus on a particular group of children, whose 'loss' stems only indirectly from the behaviour of a parent. This marks a difference from most situations because typically loss in childhood is perceived to stem from parental death or desertion; in other words, the child is orphaned. Even when it is associated with divorce or legal separation of parents, loss is 'caused' directly by parental action. But there are other situations which lead to loss in childhood where parents have only a very partial or indirect role.

One such is where children are removed from their family by social workers – perhaps against parental wishes – in circumstances which lead to separation not only from parents but from brothers and sisters; hence there could be a sibling loss. In such situations there is a statutory obligation on professionals, committees and courts to act in the best interests of the child and to promote the child's welfare even if, in practice, such interests are not always clear-cut or uncontentious.

There are other situations, however, where there is no obligation to consider the interests of children. If a father or a mother is at risk of imprisonment, there is no requirement on the court to consider the welfare of any children involved. The emphasis is on the convicted person as an individual; the consequences of the imprisonment for other family members are not a consideration. As a result, children are sometimes deprived of a parent – perhaps a lone parent – for substantial periods.

It is the aim of this chapter to explore the implications for children of a father's imprisonment and to draw on a small scale research exercise which sought 'consumer feed-back' on a children's visits scheme at a maximum security prison. The scheme assumes, *inter alia*, that fathers are important to their children and that there is positive value/advantage in maintaining contact.

Importance of fathers

The evidence for this has not been given very much prominence. The focus of research into child development has persistently emphasised the central role of the mother/mother substitute. While this is understandable, the relevance of the father should obviously not be ignored, and increasingly studies of children are including a range of family members in identifying influences upon child development.

Lewis et al. (1981) pointed out that the early attachment literature (e.g. Bowlby 1969) had limitations: 'the young child's social, affective and intellectual development is not determined solely by the mother–infant relationship'. They argued that the attachment theories of Bowlby (1969) and Ainsworth (1969) 'assume an epigenetic model of development', i.e. there is 'a linear relationship between the infant's primary relationship with the mother, and subsequent relationships that follow. The model holds that subsequent social relations (peers in particular, but also fathers) are dependent on the initial attachment relationship between mother and infant' (p.261). For Lewis et al., the child's 'functional social relationships between different systems remain relatively independent [and] are formed simultaneously rather than sequentially, satisfying multiple and differential social needs' (p262).

In his review of research literature, Lamb (1981) failed to confirm from empirical studies in the USA the existence of monotropy; rather, infants 'clearly do become attached to both of their parents at about the same time', though they appear to prefer their mothers prior to 2 years of age, when distressed (p.13). Paternal influences on child development are bound to vary widely as, indeed, does the nature and intensity of the father–child relationship itself. This is not the place to make a further comprehensive review, but a summary of the range of effects illustrates the potential importance of fathers in this context. Research, cited by Lamb (1981), related paternal activity to sex role development, moral development, achievement and intellectual development, social competence and psychological adjustment. These factors were identified in studies both of father involvement and of father absence. Lamb concludes from this review of North American research that 'fathers and mothers both appear to be psychologically salient to their children from the time the children are infants and they appear to adopt different roles from this point on. Mothers are consistently assigned responsibility for nurturance and physical child care, whereas fathers tend to be associated with playful interaction as well as with demands that children conform to cultural norms. Fathers do appear to be more demanding and exacting'. Lamb also added that 'whether or not they have more influence on them, fathers are more involved in the socialization of sons than of daughters'.

To add to this brief catalogue, Snarey (1993) followed up after four decades the subjects studied by the Gluecks in the late 1930s. He concluded that fathers contributed to their children's 'educational and occupational mobility', i.e. to their 'success' as young adults.

The relationships of imprisoned fathers and their children has not been the subject of specific study. Suggestive related evidence, however, is provided by Lewis and O'Brien (1987). The researchers created a Non-Custodial Parent Involvement rating for divorced fathers, based on the extent to which they shared social, recreational or educational activities with their children. Involvement was positively correlated with abstract reasoning, mathematics and self-esteem in school (p.222). They conclude that 'keeping fathers involved with children is probably important for the children's well-being. Non-custodial fathers do matter to children'. (p.223)

There is certainly evidence from British studies of the impact on families of a father's imprisonment. For example, Roger Shaw has studied and written extensively on prisoners' families; he estimated (in 1987) that '100,000 children in England and Wales are annually affected by the loss of their father into prison'. In a later publication he calculated that approximately half a million children under 16 years of age will have 'experienced' their father being in prison (Shaw, 1992). While some children 'positively bloom when a violent, selfish or hurtful' member of the family is removed, Shaw (1987) found that many times the prisoners' wives whom he interviewed 'explained with bitterness' that they and their children – not their husbands – were 'serving the sentence'.

Further and more recent studies have documented and extended evidence about the impact on children of a father's imprisonment and of the benefits to be gained by appropriate parent/child contact (see, for example Lloyd, 1991). Peart and Asquith (1992) studied Scottish prisoners and their families. They report how 'partners have to cope with children who grieve for their father; who miss him but get upset when visiting in prison; who fantasise about the missing parent; and who show all the signs of loss and confusion at home but who "are as good as gold" when they go up to visit him'.

They conclude that 'for most children imprisonment of a parent is a traumatic experience and can involve the child in a changing set of family dynamics at a time when the family is likely to be experiencing severe financial hardship. Feelings of loss and confusion may well be compounded by the altered financial and emotional resources of the remaining parent or carer' (p.21). As a result, 'The emphasis should shift from re-establishing family contact to maintaining family contact.' (p.22)

Operationalising these contacts appropriately has posed new problems for those involved in and concerned for prisoners' welfare and that of their families. Because of concerns about children's need, as well as prisoners' anxiety, early in 1991 Holloway Prison began a pilot initiative for children to visit their imprisoned mothers in a scheme which operated on alternate Sundays. Within months the scheme had become an established feature, such was its success (Lloyd 1992). Undoubtedly the Holloway venture showed that better visiting arrangements for children and families could be of value to all the parties involved.

The Woolf Report (1991) anticipated the definitive outcome of the Holloway experience with its recommendation that 'the Prison Service should consider extended visits from children to their parents in male prisons if the experiments in female establishments are successful'.

In fact this reflects and expands Prison Service Standing Order No. 5.

It is one of the roles of the Prison Service to ensure that the socially harmful effects of an inmate's removal from normal life are so far as possible minimised and that his [sic] contacts with the outside world are maintained. Outside contacts are therefore encouraged especially between an inmate and his family and friends.

Of course, there are other perspectives on this situation beyond that of the inmate; partners must maintain contact if any kind of meaningful relationship is to be sustained against the time of the inmate's release; further, as discussed above, children have their own needs for contact, needs which are reflected in the United Nation's Convention on the Rights of Children (1989). *Inter alia* these include a declaration that all rights apply equally to all children without exception and that the State has an obligation to protect children from any form of discrimination or punishment ' . . . on the basis of the . . . activities . . . of the child's parents' (Article 2); moreover, the State should 'respect the right of the child who is separated from one or both parents to maintain personal relations and direct contact with both parents on a regular basis, except if it is contrary to the child's best interests.' (Article 9)

Understandably, the Prison Service has to concentrate much of its resources of all kinds on ensuring the security of establishments and the protection of the public; it has also long recognized an obligation to inmates in its charge. Increasingly, because of legislation and international declarations, it is needing to take into account the rights of children in its provision and this is no easy objective to achieve, given the uneasy balance of interests of all parties – coupled with the overriding concern for security. Such aims and such concerns raise particularly acute issues in a maximum security prison and for the children of men serving a long term of imprisonment. Given the constraints imposed by prison security, if a scheme were instituted to enable imprisoned fathers to be involved more fully with their children, would prisoners and their families take advantage of it? If so, would it be possible for a meaningful and worthwhile relationship of father and child to develop or be sustained?

The Ormiston Charitable Trust, which operates a range of children's projects in East Anglia, believed that such questions should be tested out in practice.

Children's visits at HMP Whitemoor

After discussions with prison staff a scheme for children's visits was established in the newly opened Whitemoor Prison. As documented in Wedge (1995) the prison took its first inmates in 1991 and holds just over 500 men, most of whom are serving more than six years. About half of the inmates are 'vulnerable prisoners' (V.P.s), segregated from the main body of prisoners in view of the nature of their offence and/or to protect them from possible violence. In HMP Whitemoor, these vulnerable prisoners are so numerous that they are accommodated in a specialist unit comprising two self-contained 'wings' which operate a regime designed specifically for the management of the V.P.s.

The Ormiston Charitable Trust manages the Visitors' Centre and a crèche located at one end of the visits hall. Children's visits are held every Tuesday afternoon and are intended exclusively for up to ten families with at least one child under twelve years of age. The visits are explained in the Trust's leaflet, available in the Visitors' Centre:

> The purpose of children's visits is to enable the inmate to maintain the special relationship he has with his children. To encourage this, Ormiston staff arrange toys, games and activities, board games etc. The inmate is free to move around the room with his children, taking part in any activity they choose. Spontaneous activities are also encouraged, e.g. piggy-back rides.

The general impression by mid-1993 was that the children's visits were an important innovation, much appreciated by those involved – inmates, children, partners and prison staff. There were, however, people with reservations. Moreover, the take-up of this relatively expensive provision was often disappointing, prompting questions in the Trust and in the prison about appropriateness and about value for money. It was a situation which suggested the need for a systematic review to address some of these issues as well as to ascertain the level of 'consumer satisfaction' to inform decisions about possible improvements. The commission to undertake a study was accepted by the University of East Anglia where the School of Social Work has a long record of research into both child care needs and work with offenders.

The research

It seemed to all parties that the most useful function of a study would be to obtain the views of representatives of the groups of participants in the Whitemoor scheme – inmates, prison staff and visitors. Additionally, views could be obtained from inmates who, though eligible, had declined to take advantage of children's visits entirely, or had ceased to do so after having experienced one or more visits; another group offering insight would be users of the visits who had been transferred away from Whitemoor to a prison where such visits were not available.

It was not practicable to seek objective data about the impact of visits on children's development or on parent–child relationships. The principal focus was to establish the response and attitudes of the various actual and potential 'consumers' as well as those responsible for the provision. In this present account the focus is on the reactions of inmates and visitors. Other details can be found in Wedge (1995).

The data reported here came from interviews which took place with various categories of people:

a) all inmates who had received four or more children's visits were seen on their wing ('Users')
b) a random sample of inmates who had used the visits between one and three times but appeared to have stopped doing so were also seen on their wing ('Ex-users')
c) a random sample of inmates who had never used children's visits but whose apparently eligible children came to ordinary visits were similarly seen on their wing ('Non-users')
d) some inmates who had been moved from Whitemoor after making extensive use of children's visits were seen in their 'new' establishment ('Moved users')
e) visitors using children's visits were interviewed in the Visitors' Centre; these were mainly parents/carers, but on occasion older children also participated ('Visitor users')
f) visitors not using children's visits were similarly interviewed in the Visitors' Centre ('Visitor non-users')

Altogether there were 55 interviews of prisoners, 16 of visitors, (see detailed figures below) conducted in 1994.

Findings

a) General

It should be remembered that the findings represent views obtained at a particular stage in the evolution and development of the Children's Visits scheme. Also, the operational arrangements reflect the particular prison circumstances, notably a new, maximum security institution for over 500 inmates with towards half of the complement being vulnerable prisoners. In fact, in equipping the visits room the opportunity was taken to choose furniture

119

which could encourage more natural physical contact during visits. Low coffee tables and fabric-covered chairs facilitate a more informal atmosphere compared with the more usual cafe-type tables and plastic/wooden chairs.

The numbers of interviewees was as follows:

Inmates		Matched Visitor families
Users	19	5
Ex-Users	5	1
Non-Users	9	5
Moved-Users	6	–
Total	39	11

		Unmatched Visitor families
		5
	Total	16

While the numbers involved in any one category are small, the views put forward can be seen to reflect a spread of opinion, as the detailed results indicate.

b) The visitors

i   *The families.* The 19 users had 52 children, the 9 non-user inmates had 24; unless an inmate had more than one family, all the eligible children tended to come to visits. For 35 of the 39 inmates interviewed, the child was brought by the wife, or the partner, or the mother of the child; a few children were brought by a grandparent or other relative; one visiting child was accompanied by a social worker/probation officer, and one by a foster parent.

ii   *The journey.* The inmates and visitors were asked about the distance travelled to Whitemoor and/or the time away from home when coming on a visit. Only seven families made a round trip of less than 150 miles or took less than six hours; at the other extreme, seven families travelled over 250 miles or were away from home for more than twelve hours in making a visit of about two hours. This suggests a high level of commitment to visiting, a commitment confirmed by an examination of the frequency of coming to Whitemoor. Of the seven families travelling over 250 miles, or taking more than twelve hours, two visited fortnightly. Generally, there was no clear evidence that distance or time taken was related to frequency of visiting, or to mode of transport (i.e. whether public or private).

c) The inmates

i   *Ordinary visits.* All inmates using children's visits also used ordinary visits; most of the ex-users did the same. Also, since many eligible inmates did not use children's visits it was important to establish opinions of ordinary visits. The focus was on arrangements for children.

- When asked what was liked and disliked about ordinary visits there was some appreciation of the crèche facility and of the visit helping to maintain family links. On the negative side, four issues predominated:

  There was very strong feeling about the mixture of 'ordinary' and vulnerable prisoners on visits; vulnerable prisoners and their families felt that the physical location of the crèche in the visits room was too distant from them; there was concern at boredom experienced by older children; a number of inmates and visitors complained about the lack of family privacy and the high level of surveillance, as they perceived it.

- Those not using children's visits were asked the reason for their failing to avail themselves of them. Of the nine non-users, seven referred to Tuesday being a school day and therefore inappropriate; for three inmates and two of the matched visitors the reason given was the mixing of ordinary and vulnerable prisoners. This feeling between the two groups of prisoners was expanded upon by one inmate who referred to tension spilling out after the ordinary visit (where the groups are segregated though in the same room) and hostility being directed at families; as a vulnerable prisoner he was particularly conscious of this and appreciated the mixing of the two categories of prisoner on children's visits which he found to be much more relaxed.

ii *Children's visits.* There was a high degree of appreciation of these children's visits, which were described as 'good' or 'excellent' by many. Inmates and their families welcomed the additional freedom of movement they afforded and the relaxed atmosphere. Not surprisingly, father–child activities were specifically mentioned positively. Three of the inmate users could think of no criticism.

- One father remarked: 'I like to be physical with my children and children's visits mean my [nine year old] daughter can move about freely and we can play together.'

  More than one inmate referred to their responsibility as a father. For example, 'I like the contact with my children. It's important for me to go on exercising my responsibility even though I'm in prison.'

121

Another spoke of 'being able to play as a family. It helps bonding between [my daughter aged two years] and me, and it helps in maintaining our relationship. I feel involved in her development'.

- There was an overwhelming view among the inmates that the whole family benefitted from children's visits, not just the child or the inmate. (Rarely was there any 'loser'.) One father spoke in detail as follows:

> The children benefit from seeing me in a fairly normal environment, and I benefit the same; it's like being a normal family for a short time. It makes me feel more secure as a father, that family relationships are intact. I wouldn't have had the same relationship with [my daughter aged three years] if I hadn't had children's visits. She was born three weeks after I came to prison and at the first two prisons she could only sit on my knee for half an hour, as opposed to playing and getting to know one another at length. Now I feel we're very close; it's almost as if I've never been away when she comes to see me now. And my wife's benefitted from the change of emphasis of being a 'single' parent to being able to involve me as a father as well. I feel the opportunity to be a 'normal' family has cemented our relationship.

One visitor said she was barely pregnant when the inmate was imprisoned. 'He has never been at home with our [young son, aged two years]. Children's visits have meant [the inmate] could develop contact and a relationship with the baby. The child benefits because he knows who his father is – and it helps me to manage him at home'.

- These kinds of sentiments lay behind many of the responses of interviewees when asked what had persuaded them to use children's visits. The most common answer referred to 'helping the family to survive', 'cohesiveness', 'benefitting from a special kind of visit', 'closer contact with my child'. Also there were again various comments on having more freedom of movement and being more relaxed. One inmate expressed his positive feelings by remarking that 'No persuasion was needed' (to continue to use children's visits).

Another used the visits 'because I enjoy the less restrictive contact with my [three] children and I think this kind of contact helps the mothers cope better with the children outside the prison. She can say to our children that if they misbehave I'll deal with the matter on the next visit; this seems to be effective both for [mother] and in my exercise of parental control'.

One inmate reflected, 'I can spend time reading with the children, can play with them and I can talk with the older ones. It's very

122

important to maintain family links, and children's visits help to do this. Two hours is still a short time to divide between family members though; it's inadequate. I'd like to spend longer.'

- Inmates and visitors were also asked what would/did put them off using children's visits. For the vast majority of users the answer was that nothing would deter them; a small minority, however, referred to 'more surveillance', 'increased security arrangements' or 'searching my family'. Among ex-users there was a range of responses; 'too much surveillance' recurred and for some the atmosphere was 'not relaxed'; they were 'unable to behave normally with the family'. One inmate ceased to use children's visits because of school attendance on Tuesdays.
- Almost all inmates and visitors expressed similar views about their feelings before, during and after visits. In advance there is anticipation and excitement; during the visits there is enjoyment and afterwards depression – feeling dreadful/terrible, low, sad/lonely.
- Finally, the reaction of the children was again expressed positively by most inmates and visitors. They were said to have been happy and to have enjoyed themselves during the visits even though a number were upset or fractious afterwards.

Discussion

There are some significant general points to be made before considering specifically the attachment of children to their imprisoned fathers. First, none of those interviewed suggested that children's visits were other than a good institution and the users were very positive about them. The reasons given reflected a very appreciative welcome of the enhanced contact between father and child which such visits promoted and enabled. Despite gender stereotyping, which prison life can be expected to consolidate, here were men acknowledging and discussing the discharging of their caring paternal role.

Secondly, discharging such a role through active involvement with one's child during children's visits meant for the inmates both the rejection of any 'macho' exhibitionism which might be a necessary part of behaviour with others on the wing, and also the assumption of a more tender manner, more suited to a gentler existence outside prison. Though not specifically asked, no interviewee volunteered any negative or hostile view about this shift, or hinted at unwanted comment from fellow inmates – or for that matter from staff. It would seem that the prison culture accepted this 'softer' element in the context of visits involving children.

Thirdly, it is entirely possible that many inmates were more conscious of their paternal role when inside prison than when outside in the community. (Of course, this could also be true of their role as husband/partner.) At the least, prison affords time for thought and for reflection; for many, it sharpens awareness above all of the importance of personal relationships to individual identity and the deep loss threatened by incarceration. For the inmate, visits offer a chance to renew, maintain or revive some of those relationships. For that reason visits can be invested with massive emotional anticipation; in practice they do not always justify that investment. The partner and children could be pre-occupied with quite different issues from those concerning the inmate. Besides, for most of the period of sentence they might be trying to cope with serious difficulties in their daily lives, difficulties often exacerbated if not entirely caused, by the man's imprisonment.

Fourthly, given these factors, regular children's visits are potentially very important. They offer an opportunity to ensure an emphasis on maintaining rather than re-establishing family contact (Peart and Asquith, 1992) and to promote children's well-being by keeping fathers involved with them (Lewis & O'Brien, 1987).

Turning to more specific issues revealed in the interviews, it is possible to identify what children's visits appear to have contributed to securing the father–child relationship; the responses also afford an insight into perceptions of fatherhood and the exercise of the paternal role.

i 'Knowing my child'

There were some respondents whose child had been born after they had been taken into custody. One mother reported not only that the children's visits enabled the father to 'develop contact and a relationship with the baby' but also that 'the child benefits because he knows who his father is'. A father whose child was born a few weeks after imprisonment compared the limited contact in other establishments with the ability at HMP Whitemoor 'to get to know one another at length'. He continued by reflecting that without children's visits he 'wouldn't have had the same relationship' with his daughter.

Clearly for these families it was important for father and child to know one another. Without such 'knowledge' a meaningful relationship would become even more problematic. Indeed, another inmate referred explicitly to activity during children's visits as helping 'bonding' between his two year old daughter and himself, and added 'it helps in maintaining our relationship. I feel involved in her development'.

These inmates might not have read widely about child development but nevertheless reflected appreciatively on their experience using words and concepts like 'contact', 'knowing', 'bonding' and 'maintaining our relationship'.

ii Parental responsibility

Reference has already been made to inmates mentioning their ability to 'exercise' paternal responsibility 'even though in prison'. Another spoke of his wife being 'able to involve me as a father' and being 'more secure as a father'. One inmate saw himself continuing as the family authority figure in his 'exercise of parental control' at a distance because his wife could warn the children that he would deal with misbehaviour on the next visit.

This last example describes an explicit form of parental responsibility and probably is by no means unique among prisoners' families. For the purpose of this account, however, it is but one among a number in which inmates welcome the opportunity to discharge their paternal function in respect of their children. We do not know the child's perception; it can be expected however that their father will be no remote, anonymous figure but perhaps a significant person in their life even though not at home with them and their mother.

iii Physical play

There was much comment from our interviewees about the enjoyment and apparent importance of play with their children. One prisoner spoke of liking to be 'physical' with his children, with whom he was able to play together during children's visits. Another spoke of 'being able to play as a family'. There was also an interviewee who said that during children's visits he would spend time reading, playing and talking with his children because it was 'very important to maintain family links'.

The extent and type of participation in play activity varied widely on children's visits but the fathers who were interviewed reflected positively on this opportunity. Of course, play materials were provided and the whole ethos of the visits encouraged play as a vehicle for establishing or sustaining father–child relationships. Those who were interviewed, however, were not commenting on their own pleasure at being able to play. On the contrary, play was experienced by them as a means for developing and expressing the father's closeness with his child. It fitted well with the evidence reported in Lamb (1981) that fathers tend to be associated with playful interaction, in contrast to mothers; in the Whitemoor setting however, it was a relationship through play that was made available, not play itself. The inmates using the facility recognized this and responded accordingly.

iv Family survival

Without being over-dramatic, eight of the nineteen 'users' referred to the experience of children's visits as 'helping the family to survive' or helping 'cohesiveness'. Through closer involvement with the children, these inmates saw themselves contributing directly to the children's development and indirectly to the support of the mother. At least one inmate referred explicitly to the more relaxed atmosphere of children's visits being a contributory factor

125

in sustaining a marriage. This was a man who had been moved to another establishment where visits were more conventional and therefore more tense compared with those at Whitemoor. When interviewed he was involved in divorce proceedings and observed that this 'might have been avoided with the Whitemoor arrangements'. His current facilities were 'not sufficiently relaxed for a proper expression of feelings'.

Conclusions

Although very large numbers of children experience their father being in prison (Shaw, 1987 and 1992) only a relatively small proportion of the men concerned will have been sentenced for a long term. Nevertheless, the absolute number of children involved is substantial. Moreover, even a short-term prison sentence can represent a long period on a child's time-scale. In fact, the interviews reported here were with men whose length of imprisonment was at the upper end of the range and who were currently serving their sentence in a maximum security establishment. The seriousness of their crimes had prompted judicial action separating them from their families for more than six years (by definition); obviously, in such circumstances children face a potential loss of attachment with the attendant risk of emotional and behavioural disturbance which can compound the other difficulties faced by prisoners' families (e.g. Peart and Asquith, 1992).

The evidence from this small-scale study of one scheme is encouraging for the children taking part.

1   With relevant commitment it is possible to devise and operate children's visits successfully in a maximum security prison, despite the inevitable emphasis on that maximum security.
2   The participating fathers believe themselves to be important to their children; this is a belief which should not necessarily be assumed. In fact, by their responses, the prisoners who were interviewed intuitively confirmed in general terms evidence from research (e.g. Lamb 1981; Snarey 1993). By the reports of their actions they certainly support the conclusion of Lewis and O'Brien (1987) that the involvement of a (non-custodial) father matters to children.
3   The belief in the value of prisoner-father involvement is shared by the partners of the men concerned. Apart from comments made when interviewed, some of the mothers not only visited very regularly but also undertook long and sometimes very inconvenient journeys with their children.
4   Among the benefits afforded prisoner-fathers by the children's visits scheme, those interviewed referred to four particular functions of fatherhood which the visits enabled or enhanced. These were that they could

'get to know' their children, could discharge 'parental responsibility', could indulge in play and could 'support' the family. At both a general and a specific level, each of these functions contributes to the psychological attachment of the younger family members with the potential advantages which that can imply.

5   These advantages cannot compensate wholly for the long-term absence of the father from the family home, but the visits are certainly perceived by the prisoner-fathers in terms which suggest that some mitigation occurs. Fathers believe that they can establish and sustain meaningful – if partial – relationships despite their long-term imprisonment.

6   To return to the beginning of this process, it is unlikely that sentencing will ever take into account the family circumstances of fathers. Indeed, it could be argued that to do so would be inequitable – particularly for those convicted of more serious offences. Yet it is among families of the more serious offenders that the problem of maintaining contact is likely to be most acute. We can expect that children whose fathers are imprisoned for particularly long periods will nevertheless benefit from continued contact, provided that contact allows the development and/or maintenance of a meaningful relationship.

7   The evidence from the interviews with inmates of HMP Whitemoor suggests that appropriate schemes can be established in the prison system. Such a scheme can of course be of considerable help to the prisoners in various ways, for example in tolerating prison life, contributing to appropriate role-taking on release. Particularly, though, such schemes can lead to better father–child relationships, can sustain an element of attachment, can reduce the extent of loss and by extension, improve children's development with the potential advantages which that can bring for the individual and society.

8   This implies that schemes specifically intended to embrace good father–child contact among inmates should be actively promoted and developed generally. If a children's visits scheme can be established in a maximum security prison, then appropriate arrangements should surely be possible in other types of establishments. The interest shown in the project at HMP Whitemoor and the initiatives taken in some other prisons suggest that the value of special schemes for children is being increasingly recognized. It is to be hoped that by these means, loss in childhood which results from judicial action will be significantly reduced among prisoners' families generally.

Acknowledgements

The research reported in this chapter was made possible by funding from the Ormiston Charitable Trust which is gratefully acknowledged, as is the help of

Ormiston staff. Thanks are also due to all the inmates and visitors who were interviewed, to Prison Service managers and to staff at HMP Whitemoor for their willing co-operation and participation. Finally, I owe a large debt to my research colleagues, Avril Price and Dr. Gwyneth Boswell.

References

Ainsworth, M.D.S. (1969). 'Object relation, dependency and attachment: a theoretical review of the infant–mother relationship'. *Child Development* 40. 969–1026.

Bowlby, J. (1969). *Attachment and Loss. Vol. 1 Attachment*. New York: Basic Books.

Home Office (1991). 'Report of an inquiry into prison disturbances April 1990 by the Rt. Hon. Lord Woolf and His Honour Judge Stephen Tumin'.

Lamb, M. E. (1981). 'Fathers and child development' in Lamb, M.E. (ed.) *The Role of the Father in Child Development*. New York: John Wiley.

Lewis, C. and O'Brien, M. (1987). *Reassessing Fatherhood*. London: Sage.

Lewis, M., Feiring, C. and Weinraub, M. (1981). 'The father as a member of the child's social network' in Lamb, M. E. (ed.) *The Role of the Father in Child Development*. New York: John Wiley.

Lloyd, E. (1991). 'Contact between children and their imprisoned parents: research and practice'. Prison Service Psychology Conference Proceedings.

Lloyd, E. (ed) (1992). *Children Visiting Holloway Prison*. Save the Children Fund.

Peart, K. and Asquith, S. (1992). *Scottish Prisoners and their Families*. Save the Children Fund, Edinburgh.

Shaw, R. (1987). *Children of Imprisoned Fathers*. Hodder and Stoughton.

Shaw, R. (ed) (1992). *Prisoners' Children*. London: Routledge.

Snarey, J. (1993). *How Fathers Care for the Next Generation*. Harvard University Press.

U.N. General Assembly (1989). *Convention on the Rights of the Child*. U.N. New York.

Wedge, P. (1995). *A report on children's visits to imprisoned fathers: the scheme at HMP Whitemoor*. Ipswich: Ormiston Trust.

8 Psychological parenting and child placement: 'But we want to have our cake and eat it'

June Thoburn

The concept of 'psychological parenting' as applied to child placement

This chapter is concerned with children who, for a large part of their child-hood, are looked after by parents other than those to whom they were born. A brief review of 'permanence policies' will provide the context for a con-sideration of the ways in which theories of child development and attachment have an impact on decisions about placement and about social work practice.

A historical perspective on child placement theory and practice over the last forty years or so, shows that there has been a tension between an emphasis on the importance of the family of origin to the child – sometimes referred to as an emphasis on the 'blood tie' – and an emphasis on 'psychological parent-ing' – that is, the provision of a stable nurturing environment, preferably by the birth parents but otherwise by substitute parents (see Thoburn et al., 1986 and Thoburn, 1992, for a fuller discussion of these concepts). This debate is sometimes conceptualised in terms of parents' rights versus children's rights, but the swings in policy and practice have been more between parent's rights or wishes, and the rights and preferences of substitute parents. It is only recently, in particular with the implementation of the England and Wales Children Act 1989, that the wishes of the children themselves have been given greater prominence when decisions are made about their future.

Other contributors to this volume have summarised the evidence for the importance of continuity of relationships with at least one caring adult for the growing child's healthy physical, intellectual and emotional development. It is these theories which lie at the heart of the 'permanence movement' which dominated British and American child placement practice in the late 1970s and 1980s. In both countries, researchers, clinical practitioners and child placement workers concluded that children were being harmed by an over-emphasis on parental rights which resulted in them experiencing multiple moves, usually unplanned, if their parents were unable to provide them with continuity of care. The term 'yo-yo children' was coined for those who moved

129

between carers in their family or neighbourhood, or moved in and out of public care (NSPCC, 1974) and the term 'drifting in care' was extensively applied to those who remained in foster care or children's homes for a long period without being sure whether any particular home was meant to be a permanent one, and often exposed to a series of short term placements which ended precipitately (Rowe and Lambert, 1973; Vernon and Fruin, 1986). Some of these children settled in substitute families despite the lack of legal security, only to be involved in what became known as 'tug of love' battles when they were reclaimed by parents who had for periods of years disappeared from their lives.

The writings of Goldstein, Freud and Solnit (1973 and 1979) were particularly influential in providing a theoretical framework for the change in practice sanctioned by the Children Act 1975. This legislation made it more possible to sever the legal rights of the families of origin so that children could be placed with permanent substitute families, preferably for adoption, against the wishes of their parents. Also important was the work of child placement specialists, mainly based within adoption agencies, who demonstrated that adoptive parents could be found for children who were past infancy and may have been exposed to harmful experiences.

Although these substitute parents were told about the possible, indeed likely, adverse impact of deprivation and the disruption of early relationships on the children's behaviour, the emphasis tended to be on problems in the early stages after placement. In much of the literature of that time there is an optimism about the positive impact of being brought up in a loving and secure environment, and the likelihood that early harm will be reversible in most cases. Such optimism is expressed in the title of a collection of papers 'No Child Is Unadoptable'. Clinicians such as Vera Fahlberg (1988), child placement workers in agencies such as Spaulding for Children in USA (Donley, 1975) and Parents for Children (Argent, 1984) and Barnordo's New Families projects in UK (Lindsay-Smith and Price, 1980; Fratter et al., 1982) worked out a highly influential theory of child placement practice. If children could not have a 'sense of permanence' in their family of origin, they should be placed as quickly as possible with permanent substitute parents who would become their 'psychological parents'. It was further argued that the children would not allow themselves to become attached to these new parents until they had separated from and worked through their grief at the loss of their first parents. If possible the first parents should be helped to accept that their child's future lay with substitute parents and give the children permission to attach to new parents by consenting to the adoption. Social workers and therapists were involved at this stage in undertaking 'life story work' to help the children to understand why it was necessary for them to lose one set of parents before they could move to live with a new family.

Because of the increasing emphasis on the provision of family support services for families under stress, those needing to be placed with new families had almost invariably suffered from serious adverse circumstances. A survey of 1,165 children placed between 1980 and 1985 (Thoburn and Rowe in Fratter et al., 1991) showed that over half were described as having a history of abuse or deprivation; around a third had experienced multiple moves; and just under a quarter had been placed previously in a home which was meant to be permanent but which had broken down. Few of these children will have been well-attached to their mother or father but equally few will have been totally unattached. The majority will have been ambivalently or insecurely attached. Some had already 'cut their losses' and greeted with enthusiasm the idea of a 'keeping family' where they would stay until they were grown up, be properly fed, clothed, protected from harm at the hands of their parents or others, and, in most cases be offered material benefits which they were unused to in their first families. Others resisted the idea of losing their first families but were not given that choice or were placed against their wishes. Morris (1985) describes how the social workers at the time were reluctant to hear what the children were saying if it did not accord with this dominant ideology, and Fitzgerald (1983) describes how disruptions were most likely to occur when children had not understood or accepted the need to lose contact with their first parents.

In view of our awareness through the work of Bowlby (1971) and the Robertsons (1968) of the harmful effects of separation and loss on children who are either attached or ambivalently or insecurely attached to a parenting adult, it is not entirely clear why this total severance model became the dominant ideology until one reads the literature on the recruitment of substitute families. Here the language is of the importance of the substitute parents 'claiming' the child. Influential writers such as Jewett (1978, 1984), widely read by child placement social workers and adopters, emphasised the importance of helping substitute parents to find ways to reinforce the child's attachment and sense of belonging to their family. Attention was given to the language used, particularly to helping the child to call them 'mummy and daddy'.

In reading the literature of this period it becomes clear that the emphasis on the child severing all links with the first family before placement with a substitute family is based on the belief that this was essential, not so much for the *child*, as for the *new parents*. This in turn was linked to the idea that it would not be possible to recruit adopters for these older children unless they were given a 'clear run' unimpeded by reminders of the child's first family and earlier attachments. These theories of the attachment process between adopters and older children appeared particularly relevant when involuntarily childless couples started off wanting to adopt a baby and were then encouraged to consider adopting an older child. In hindsight and with the help of research findings, it can be argued that, whilst the working hypothesis that the child's healthy development is likely to be enhanced if child and new parents have a 'sense of permanence' appears to have support in research findings, the hypothesis, coming from a crude interpretation of Goldstein et al.'s work, that contact with the first parents must be terminated so that they can have a 'clear run' at the child's emotional education has not been substantiated. As this chapter seeks to demonstrate, mutual attachments develop whether or not the adopters have exclusive tenure of the parenting role. Rowe's statement in a seminal paper in the seventies can be applied to permanent family placement in the nineties:

> The concepts of biological and psychological parenting are basic to any study of fostering relationships . . . A foster parent's role must always depend on what aspects of the parental role are still being exercised by the natural parents. (Rowe, 1977:15)

Clearly when permanent family placement is being considered, the substitute parents will take on most of the parenting roles and tasks. However the 'fit' between the respective roles, including the pattern of affectional bonds between the child and the first and the new parents, will be different in each case and will vary over time. This question of 'emotional fit' – of the possibility of dual or indeed multiple 'psychological parenting' is the focus of this chapter.

An overview of the research on permanent family placement

A series of research studies and well publicised case histories has shown that, whilst both children and their substitute parents benefit greatly from knowing that they can invest their emotional energies in each other without the fear of arbitrary removal, the apparent promise of unencumbered possession of the child, of a fresh start, which appeared to be held out by the total severance model, was a fantasy. The work on the psychology of adoption summarised by Brodzinsky and Schechter (1990) but flagged up as early as 1964 by Kirk's work on the theory of 'shared fate' and 'acceptance of difference' should have alerted workers to the likely adverse consequences of these 'rescue fantasies' and indeed a careful reading of the main protagonists of 'permanence' does not support the exclusive posession model of substitute parenting. Jane Rowe, whose authorship of *Children Who Wait* (1973) is linked by many writers with the switch in UK to 'permanence policies' summarises the research of that time as saying that:

> *all* children being brought up by people other than their birth parents do need knowledge of and sometimes access to their origins if they are to have a comfortable sense of their own identity.

Maluccio (1986: 79–80), summarising North American practice and research, highlights:

132

the crucial importance of the biological family in the growth and functioning of the child in placement . . . Workers should therefore view the
goal of preserving family ties as a major imperative in child care.

Fahlberg (1988: 198) writes in a work-book for adoption specialists:

The acceptance of birth parents and what they mean to a child's life is critical if we are to help children deal with their feelings about separation from
birth parents.

In the mid-1980s research and evaluative studies of the placement of older
children with substitute families began to appear in the USA and Britain.
(Barth and Berry, 1988, summarise the American studies, and Thoburn, 1990,
and Shaw, 1994, the British research studies). The general conclusion was
that whilst no *group* of children should be considered unadoptable in that
there are striking success stories even for children with severe behaviour
problems or disabilities, or as old as fifteen or sixteen at placement, nevertheless there were clearly some children who were not willing or not able to
settle in permanent substitute families. The average breakdown rate within up
to five years of placement was around one in five, with the proportion rising
to almost one in two when children were placed around the age of eleven or
twelve. From a survey of 1165 placements Rowe and Thoburn (in Fratter et
al., 1991) found that having experienced abuse or deprivation prior to placement was independently associated with breakdown when other variables
were held constant.

These studies suggest that early harm may sometimes be reparable by
placement with substitute parents, but that this is not invariably the case.
Qualitative studies suggest that the reason for placement breakdown is the
child's unwillingness or inability to trust and become attached to the parents
who were intended to be the new psychological parents. The older the child
at placement, the more likely was it that the placement would disrupt, but
there is evidence from clinical work, family placement workers and qualitative research studies that some children placed as toddlers were unable to
become attached to their substitute parents. Recently American writers have
coined the phase 'reactive attachment disorder' to describe the often violent,
angry, withdrawn or bizarre behaviour of these children. The adoptive parents
of a boy placed at the age of eight who were interviewed six years later said
'it's like a box; we are in one corner and he is in the other and there is nothing in between'. When interviewed two years after placement they described
their feelings as very positive and were about to proceed to adopt him. This
placement broke down three years after the adoption and shortly after this
bleak statement was made to the researcher (Thoburn, 1990).

The case illustrates that even when placements do not break down within
the research time scale which is often five years or even shorter, this does not

necessarily imply that the placement is perceived as satisfactory by the child or the substitute parents. Qualitative studies have also confirmed that even when placements do not break down, some children fail to become attached to a substitute parent and even when they do, many remain troubled about issues of identity or do not feel valued as the persons they are, but rather believe that love is offered conditionally upon their taking on a totally new identity as the child of the new family. A young woman placed at twelve whose emotional difficulties became increasingly marked left a note for her foster mother as she walked out on New Year's Eve five years later saying 'Mum, I've tried. I can't be the girl you want me to be'. Her brother aged eleven when placed in the same family, became quickly attached and made excellent progress. Quantitative studies (Barth and Berry, 1988; Fratter et al., 1991) of children placed from care have concluded that continued contact with birth parents or other members of the birth family, and being placed in the new family together with a sibling, are associated with lower breakdown rates. Qualitative studies are beginning to appear which report on why this might be so, for those placed as infants as well as for older children (Beek, 1994; Fratter, 1994).

These findings support the view that the art of child placement lies in meeting both the child's need for a sense of permanence and his or her need for a sense of personal identity and for that identity to be respected by the substitute parents. They are totally consistent with what one might expect from Bowlby's theories of a 'secure base' (Bowlby, 1988), and from the work of writers cited above on the psychology of adoption and the importance of the adopters accepting and valuing the child's dual heritage.

Research studies, and the work of practitioners who have had to pick up the pieces when placements have broken down, most notably the workers at Post Adoption Centres (Burnell, 1994), have shown that the child's and the new parents' need for a sense of permanence has to be met without doing harm to the child's sense of identity and self-concept. As a result, some child placement workers have moved away from the total severance model of placement. They attempt to offer the benefits of good quality parenting, stability and security, and if all works well, the experience of loving and being loved, without having to expose the child to unnecessary loss of relationships with the first parents, and with the added benefit of having a clear sense of identity reinforced by continued contact with the first family. This move mirrors the greater openness in baby adoption being developed in Australia and New Zealand (Mullender, 1991; Ryburn, 1994). Fratter (1991) notes that for several years it has been common for the adopters to meet members of the birth family, usually the mother, before the child was placed with them. Increasingly face to face contact between the child and the birth parents continues after placement and even when this is not possible, there is usually some sort of indirect contact such as the exchange of letters and photographs, possibly through a third party.

As with the swing towards a total severance model in the seventies, this more inclusive model of permanent family placement is also sanctioned by changes in legislation. The incorporation of these ideas into the debate leading up to the 1989 Children Act has had the following results:

- Fewer children are being placed with permanent substitute families since more effort is made to ensure that their need for both permanence and identity is met by their remaining within their families of origin.
- The requirement to make strenuous efforts to ensure that children who are looked after by the Local Authority are enabled to have comfortable contact with members of their first family has meant that, having striven to achieve this, it is illogical then to end it in order to place the child with a substitute family.

The emphasis on giving due consideration to the wishes and feelings of parents and children has meant that more are asking for substitute families to be found who will facilitate the continuation of these links. The emphasis on working in partnership has meant that when parents are persuaded, however reluctantly, that they are not able to care permanently for their children and agree with the social workers that the child therefore needs permanent substitute placement, this placement will increasingly be made without recourse to the Courts, and with the parents retaining parental responsibility until it is transferred to the adopters (or foster parents perhaps applying for a residence order). This means that their wishes about the nature of the placement, including their wishes about contact, have to be given careful consideration in the planning and placement process.

Towards a new practice theory for permanent family placement

In the light of these developments, a new theory and practice of permanent substitute placement is being developed. This theory accepts the premise that secure attachments to psychological parents are crucially important to the child's emotional development, but postulates that in some cases there may be dual or multiple psychological parenting, either for an overlapping period of time, or throughout childhood. Such a theory of child placement requires careful assessment of the child's original attachments, and of the role which the members of the first family can play after the child joins a new family, before the new family is chosen. For such an assessment to take place it is essential that high quality bridge or assessment placements are available where the child can be given affectionate and skilled care for as long as is necessary to find the substitute family whose notion of psychological parenting fits with the parenting needs of the child.

Child placement workers in the nineties are reassessing the theories of

135

permanent family placement of the seventies and eighties, and in particular the notion of the total transfer of psychological parenting from the first family to the new family. As workers become more proficient in meeting the child's parallel needs for a sense of permanence and a sense of identity, more placements are being made of children of all ages who are still to some extent attached to one or both of their parents, and possibly also to a close relative such as a grandparent or to a former foster parent or day or respite carer. In line with the requirement in the Children Act, these attachments are carefully nurtured during the early stages of the placement away from home when the child is in a temporary placement.

Some agencies and individual workers still adhere to earlier practice theories and, having achieved comfortable contact between parent and child, but decided that adoption will be in the child's interests, seek leave of the Court to terminate contact. Such workers will talk about the importance of 'grief work' with the first family and the child, helping each to come to terms with their loss as they gradually reduce the contact between the parents and child and seek to break the attachment so that the child can attach to the new family. They ask the birth parents to write 'letters for later life', and prepare the adopters for how they will talk to the child about his or her first family, the reasons why the move away was necessary ('telling'), and how they might deal with requests from the child to re-establish contact with the first family ('searching'). Post-adoption support programmes frequently have sessions on 'telling' and 'searching' and they take up a large part of preparation group content and assessment of prospective adopters (Pizey, 1994). Requests made by the child to have a reunion with the birth parents are usually resisted and the young person is told that this will be possible when they reach the age of eighteen. Sometimes in these situations indirect contact is maintained via letter but often these arrangements are allowed to lapse or the contact is one way only (between the adopters and the birth family) with the child often kept in ignorance that the exchange is occuring.

Other workers, having succeeded in achieving a situation of comfortable contact between the child and the mother, father or other person to whom he or she is fully or partially attached, have concluded that to inflict the loss on the child required by the severence model of adoption, with the accompanying traumas and the need for 'grief work' is not necessary. These workers argue that to associate something which is intended to be positive – the move to a new family, with something negative – the loss of the person who has offered continuity in the child's life, is not the best way in which to start a placement. As an interim strategy some advocate a temporary halt to contact visits to be restarted once the child has settled in with the new family and they are feeling more secure in their parenting role. However, experience indicates that if this step is taken the adopters tend to put off the 'right time' and contact is often not restarted.

Several qualitative studies have reported on the progress of these more open adoptive placements. Most frequently, by the time the children who were the subject of these earlier studies had been placed with their new families, their relationship with the birth parents had become tenuous. The child, if old enough to express an opinion, was willing to be placed and indeed wanted the benefits which stable family life could bring, but did not wish to loose contact with the birth parents. In such cases, it was clear that the continuation of a relationship with the natural parents did not impede the growth of attachment to the new parents, and indeed these have tended to say that the fact that they had not totally taken away someone else's child gave them a greater sense of entitlement to the child (Thoburn, 1990; Beek 1994; Ryburn, 1994; Fratter, 1994). Although consent to adoption made things easier, it was not essential for the benefits of contact to be felt. The following quote illustrates the point, taken from Fratter's interviews, at least eight years after placement, with eighteen adopters whose twenty-six children retained contact with birth parents after adoption. Fifteen of the young people adopted into these families and five of their birth parents were also interviewed.

Gareth and Jane [adopters] had a clear picture as to the difficulties which had led to Rachel's placement in care and Cathy's reluctance to agree to adoption. Cathy felt reassured that Rachel [adopted daughter] did not feel rejected, and commented that Gareth and Jane provided excellent care for Rachel; while Rachel herself had a very clear picture of the family history, did not 'blame' Cathy or herself, and interpreted Cathy's reluctance to agree to adoption as deriving from her concern and care. In the absence of contact there could have been less sympathetic or more distressing interpretations – a 'difficult' birth mother holding up the adoption proceedings; a 'possessive' adoptive family turning Rachel against her birth mother; and a 'rejecting' birth mother.

The children also seem to have been more willing to attach to their new families, either because they were to some extent freed from the guilt arising from their choice of the comfort of the new family over the distress of staying with the first family, or because they worried less that their first parents might be in distress or difficulty. Several children interviewed by these researchers have made it clear that, despite what social workers believe, they do not find it confusing to have the 'cake' of good parenting, at the same time as 'eating the cake' of continued contact with important people from their earlier lives. It seems to be adults, and not children, who find it problematic that a child should have two people who he or she calls 'mum' or 'dad' and who fulfil different parts of his or her parenting needs. When I suggested to Bobby, who had been in his adoptive home for four years and was fearful that his contact with his birth father might be ended, that some people thought it might be confusing to a child to have two dads, he almost shouted at me 'Well, they are wrong'. A young woman who was completely integrated into her adoptive family when interviewed by Fratter and chose to end contact with her mother when she was thirteen said: 'I might have thought the grass was greener. I knew where I stood. I knew who was the better mother. I wasn't left wondering.'

Instead of having to work on the grief reactions of the child (in reality little time has been spent on the grief of the birth parents), the efforts of social workers have been directed to helping the two sets of parents to negotiate appropriate ways for this contact to be maintained without stopping the new family from getting on with their lives together as a family. From reports of the children and their new parents, these did indeed become the psychological parents, even though the first families retained an important place in the thoughts of the children. When asked what would have happened if they had not been able to continue to see their birth parents after adoption several young people interviewed by Fratter indicated that they may not have allowed themselves to be placed. A seventeen year old said:

I'd have been annoyed. It's been pretty good to see her. If not, I'd have thought, why not?'

More recently however, as a result of the Children Act requirement to offer family support including respite care, and to work in partnership with natural families and relatives, there has been a change in the profiles of the children needing substitute placement, which will require further development of theories and skills for permanent family placement work.

Although a small number of children will still need placement who have been severely maltreated and whose attachments with their parents are anxious, ambivalent, avoidant or non-existent, more placements will in the future be needed for children who are well attached to their birth parents. Such children do not easily understand why they are not allowed to live with parents to whom they are attached. The two main groups of children needing permanent placement away from their families at the present time are children whose parents have a learning disability, or a serious mental health problem, and children whose mothers are caring and competent parents except in that they have not been able to protect them from sexual or physical abuse by a partner, or who live with men who have been convicted of sexual offences against children and are unwilling to give up those relationships. The early histories of the two groups tend to be different.

Children whose parents have learning disabilities

The children of parents with learning disabilities tend to come into care as infants or toddlers after a major attempt has been made to help the mother to parent her child appropriately. Often this has involved a heavy input of help in

138

the home, or the mother and child have been placed in a residential unit. In this way the infant has been given good enough care, and mutual attachments have begun to be formed. Often it is concluded that the mother will not be able to meet the long term needs of the child without prohibitively expensive services which may in any case be unacceptable to the parent(s), and a decision is taken, usually against the parents' wishes, that the child should be placed permanently with a substitute family. Usually the child will be placed with foster parents who will facilitate contact with the birth parents often several times a week so that the attachments are maintained until the Court decides whether the child should return home or be placed elsewhere. If this stage goes on for more than a month or so, as it often does in view of the complexities of contested proceedings, the young child will develop attachments to the bridge foster parents as well as to the birth mother, thus creating a situation where there are two psychological parents, or more if the father is also involved in the parenting. A recent case example of Mary illustrates this point.

Mary was in care herself as a teenager, having been abused by her step-father, and her mother who was a prostitute. She had learning disabilities. When she became pregnant at the age of seventeen, a child protection conference was held prior to the child's birth and a decision was taken that the child should be placed on the Child Protection Register. A Care Order was sought when Billy was born and mother and baby were cared for initially at a special residential assessment unit. Billy was a pleasant, easy baby and Mary proved, with practical help, to be a reasonably competent and loving mother. After six months she was given her own flat but was told that under no circumstances should she allow Billy to be cared for by her mother or by the man who had sexually abused her. However, Mary was unable to keep her mother away from Billy and her mother and different boyfriends were found on two occasions to be babysitting whilst Mary went out with friends. Despite a great deal of support from the family centre and a family aide, Mary became depressed, and twice left Billy on his own. On one such occasion Billy was taken into police protection and a Care Order followed.

The Local Authority told Mary that they would be seeking the Court's permission to place Billy for adoption, and that, since he was still only eighteen months old, they considered it would be best for both of them if their relationship was terminated, other than through letters from the adopters to Mary to let her know how Billy was getting on. However, until the case came to Court, he was to be placed with foster parents and Mary would be allowed to visit twice weekly for two hours on each occasion, and also to see him once a week at the family centre which they both enjoyed attending.

Mary took Billy to the foster home and got on well with the foster mother. After seven months, and before the hearing of an application to free him for adoption, the foster mother had a serious illness and Billy was moved suddenly. His mother did not on this occasion go with him to the new foster home. It was decided that this was a good time for Mary to be helped to separate from her son and contact was therefore arranged at the Family Centre once a week for a shorter period. Billy became distressed after these contacts and screamed both when he left the foster mother to go to the contact meeting and again when he left his mother to go home. Mary forcefully expressed her view that the distress was because she had not gone along with Billy when he moved to the second foster home. A planning meeting concluded that an application should be made to Court to end contact. In the meantime, the foster parent suggested that the visit should take place in the foster home and Billy's distress diminished. Contact in the foster home went well and it was clear that twelve months after the separation, Billy, now aged two and a half, was still strongly attached to his mother. The psychologist, who was asked to provide a report to support the Local Authority's application for termination of contact observed several family centre meetings. He described warm and trusting interactions between mother and son, good eye contact and appropriate physical contact. He concluded that even after this length of time Mary was still Billy's prime attachment figure. He recommended that contact should stay at its present level at least until after placement in a substitute family and that Mary should be fully involved in preparing and supporting Billy through the move. He thought it likely that once Billy had settled in, contact could be reduced to a half-day once a month.

Thus even after twelve months away from his mother, Mary was still Billy's 'psychological parent'. If the arrangement recommended by the psychologist is followed, Mary will remain the psychological parent over the transition period; there will be a period when Billy is psychologically attached to both Mary and to the adoptive mother, and this situation of dual psychological parenting will continue until Billy himself, as seems likely, transfers his attachment more strongly to the adoptive parents who will be providing him with twenty-four hour a day care.

Children whose mothers are unable to protect them from abuse

A similar situation arises with mothers who have had a good relationship with their children but who make a relationship with a man who is known to have abused other children previously. These children tend to be older than is the case when the parent has a learning disability, and to be fiercely loyal to their mothers, even if the mother's boyfriend has actually abused them. They are often pre-teenage children, anything between the ages of four and nine or ten. In the case of these older children, it is likely that the prime attachment figure will remain the mother throughout the placement in temporary foster care, and in the early stages of placement with a substitute parent. Although adoption is used as a placement of choice for children in this situation, it is clearly a very different sort of adoptive parenting from that which comes to mind when most people think about adoption. It may be that in such situations long term or permanent fostering, possibly leading to an application for a Residence Order, is a more appropriate legal status. However, Beek and Fratter describe cases where open adoption in these situations has been successful, and where for quite a protracted period the child has retained psychological attachment with the first parent(s), and gradually become more attached to the new parents. In some cases, a situation of 'dual psychological parenting' is retained; in others the birth family remains the psychological parent and the foster or adoptive parents become supplementary rather than substitute parents; and in other cases the child gradually attaches to the new parents who take on day-to-day care. They become the psychological parents and the birth parent becomes a loving and interested adult friend.

Conclusion

Placements such as those described by Fratter and that considered by the psychologist to be necessary for 'Billy' are a far cry from the total severance model, where the desire of the new parents to 'claim' the child psychologically took precedence over the child's desire (usually unexpressed or unheard) not to lose an attachment figure, the birth parent. It is closer to the long term foster care placements which Holman (1975) described as 'inclusive' and which are more often to be found in Northern Ireland where legislation places more restrictions on adoption without parental consent (Kelly and MacAuley 1992) and in other European countries such as France and Sweden where the possibility of placement for adoption against parental consent is rarely available. Whilst in Britain psychologists, therapists and placement workers have concentrated on practice which encourages adopters to come forward, and facilitates a total severance model of adoption, in Europe attention has been paid to developing a psychology of long term shared parenting with a focus on helping the child to make sense of having two sets of parents, rather than helping him or her to forget one set of parents and become fully attached to the substitute parents. This is not to advocate turning back the legislative clock, as the possibility of providing legally secure substitute family placements provides an essential safeguard for sheltering the fragile new relationships as they begin to grow. Without the promise of stability some children who have experienced multiple separations or abuse and whose birth parents can not provide the standard of parenting which is essential to their social and emotional growth will not put trust in new relationships.

However, it does require social workers and others who make and provide

141

support to adoptive and foster family placements to value the contribution made by birth parents as well as by substitute parents, even if the first set of parents can only 'care about' and have no part in the 'caring for' aspects of parenting. The result may be to reduce the emphasis placed on 'attachment' as a barometer of a successful placement. Skilled, committed, tenacious and caring twenty-four hour a day parenting may then be as valued by the social workers and new parents, as research tells us it is by the children, even if parents and child never become fully attached to each other. Though disappointment in such circumstances is inevitable, the sense of failure and self blame which many adopters describe when the placement disrupts or does not live up to their hopes, may be less in evidence.

If this more complex model of psychological parenting is followed, changes in child placement practice at the different stages with birth parents, children and adopters can be considered in terms of knowledge and skills. Such changes fit well with the values which underlie the parnership approach required by the Children Act 1989. An understanding of the multi-faceted nature of parenting which gives each child the best chance of growing into an emotionally stable and competent adult will be central if the respective contributions of the birth parent and the day-to-day parent are to be understood. The experts in any one case will be the two sets of parents and the child herself as she grows in understanding. Ryburn (1994:3) describes this as 'open' model of practice 'based on a belief that the best decisions in the lives of those who use adoption services will be the ones they make for themselves'.

Since for many birth and adoptive parents this will be a once in a lifetime experience, social workers discussing the implications of adoption with birth parents and potential substitute families will have an educative role, using a range of media including books, videos, tapes of experienced adopters and adoptees talking about their experiences, to get the lessons of research and personal experience across to those contemplating such a life-changing course of action. Therapeutic skills in working with children and birth parents will still be needed especially before a substitute family is identified and if problems arise after the child has settled in. In the middle phase, from the identification of a new family who appears to be able to meet the child's needs, including the needs for the amount of birth family contact which a full assessment indicates will be appropriate, to the stage when the pattern of the new placement is well-established, support, negotiation and mediation skills will be to the fore. Elsewhere in this volume Hinings and Wedge describe the environment and skills which can allow comfortable contact to be established and, if necessary, supervised even in the most unpromising circumstances.

There is no slide-rule for the frequency, location and length of contacts between the two families. The encouraging news is that growing numbers of adopters and birth families, inextricably linked by their affection for a child who needs them both, are working it out for themselves. Their own willingness and that of their children to take part in research and training is contributing to the development of an 'inclusive' model of permanence which will avoid for some children the anguish of having to make a 'judgement of Solomon'. Adrian (described in Thoburn, 1990:51) was an eight year old with a physical disability who was desperate to find a new family after two broken foster homes and twelve months in a children's home where he was bullied. His first 'permanent' placement broke down after eight months. He was then lucky enough to be placed with adopters who were open in their attitudes and made it possible for him to talk freely about his first family. He was placed when actual contact after adoptive placement was considred inappropriate. He has made excellent progress and found 'a family for life' with his adopters. However, as he talked to me five years after he was placed, and in the presence of his adoptive parents, his regrets at the loss of his first family with whom he would have liked to have stayed in contact were painfully obvious.

Just lately – I don't know why it is – I keep having dreams. I wonder what my mum's doing now. How my dad's doing. What my sisters are doing. My mum has blond hair and is tall. My dad is like me. I just think – Oh, how it would have been nice if they liked me more. I could have seen them. I would have liked to have done. If they'd given me a bit more of a chance than I had. In my dreams, sometimes I feel a bit sad for my mum and dad, because if they had given me more time, I thought, I could have planned my future. I see pictures in my dreams of what I would have liked to have done with my sisters.

References

Argent, H. (1984), *Find me a Family*, London: Souvenir Press.
Barth, R. and Berry, M. (1988) *Adoption and Disruption: rates, risk and responses*, New York: Aldine de Gruyter.
Beek, M. (1994) 'The reality of fact-to-face contact after adoption', *Adoption and Fostering*, 18:2
Bowlby, J. (1971) *Attachment and Loss*, Harmondsworth: Penguin.
Bowlby, J. (1988) *A Secure Base*, London: Tavistock
Brodzinsky, D. and Schechter, D. (Eds.) (1990) *The Psychology of Adoption*, Oxford: Oxford University Press.
Burnell, A. (1993) 'Open adoption: A post-adoption perspective' in Adcock, M., Kaniuk, J and White, R. (Eds.) *Exploring Openness in Adoption*, Croydon: Significant Publications.
Donley, K. (1975) *Opening New Doors*, London: ABAA.
Fahlberg, V. (1988) *Fitting the Pieces Together*, London: BAAF.
Fitzgerald, J. (1983) *Understanding Disruption*, London: BAAF.
Fratter, J. (1994) *Perspectives on Adoption with Contact: Implications for*

Policy and Practice, University of Cranfield PhD thesis.

Fratter, J., Rowe, J., Sapsford, D. and Thoburn, J. (1991) *Permanent Family Placement: a Decade of Experience*, London: BAAF.

Goldstein, J., Freud, A. and Solnit, A. (1973) *Beyond the Best Interests of the Child*, New York: Free Press.

Goldstein, J., Freud, A. and Solnit, A. (1979) *Before the Best Interests of the Child*, New York: Free Press.

Jewett, C. (1984), *Helping Children Cope with Separation and Loss*, London: Batsford/BAAF.

Kelly, G. and McCauley, C. (1992) *Long term Foster Care in Northern Ireland*, Queens University Belfast.

Kirk, H.D. (1964) *Shared Fate*, London: Collier-Macmillan.

Kirk, H.D. (1981) *Adoptive Kinship: A modern institutuion in need of reform*, Vancouver: Butterworths.

Lindsay-Smith, C. and Price, E. (1980) *Barnardos New Families Project – Glasgow: The first two years*, London: Barnardos.

Maluccio, A.N., Fein, E. and Olmstead, K.A. (1986) *Permanency Planning for Children: Concepts and Methods*, London: Tavistock.

Morris, C. (1984), *The Permanency Principle in Child Care Social Work*, Norwich: SWT/UEA Social Work Monographs.

Mullender, A. (ed.) (1991) *Open Adoption*, London: BAAF.

Pizey, C. (1994) 'Issues of identity and loss in the preparation and assessment of prospective adopters of young children' *Adoption and Fostering*, 18:2.

Robertson, J. and Robertson, J. (1977) 'The Psychological Parent' *Adoption and Fostering*, 1.1 pp.19–22.

Rowe, J. and Lambert, L. (1973) *Children Who Wait*, London: ABAA.

Rowe, J. (1977) *Adoption in the Seventies*, London: BAAF.

Ryburn, M. (1994) 'Adoptive parents and contested adoption' in Ryburn, M. (ed) *Contested Adoption Proceedings*, Aldershot: Gower.

Ryburn, M. (1994) *Open Adoption: Research, Theory and Practice*, Aldershot: Avebury

Sawbridge, P., (1983) *Parents for Children. Twelve practice papers*, London: BAAF.

Shaw, M. (1994) *A Bibliography of Family Placement Literature*, London: BAAF.

Thoburn, J. (1990) *Success and Failure in Permanent Family Placement*, Aldershot: Gower.

Thoburn, J. (1992) *Child Placement: Principles and Practice*, Aldershot: Gower.

Thoburn, J., Murdoch, A. and O'Brien, A. (1986) *Permanence in Child Care*, Oxford: Blackwell.

Triseliotis J. et al. (1991) *Adoption and fostering* Report to the Scottish Office on the outcome of permanent family placements in two Scottish Local Authorities, Edinburgh: Scottish Office.

Vernon, J. and Fruin, D. (1986), In Care: *A Study of Social Work Decision Making*, London: National Children's Bureau.

9   Care leavers and their babies

Kate Pearson

The aim of the study described in this Chapter was to explore the experiences of young women who became mothers whilst being looked after by a Social Services Department, paying particular attention to their attachments, their views of the emotional support they received and how this affected their early relationships with their babies. The views of five young women were obtained using focused interviews.

The term 'in care' is used for young people who are either accommodated or the subjects of care orders. Although this term is now somewhat out-of-date and has been replaced by 'looked after', young people themselves continue to use the term 'in care'. The term 'care leavers' indicates young people between the ages sixteen and eighteen who move out of local author-ity-provided placements, not those reaching the statutory leaving care date of their eighteenth birthday.

Several influences have converged to stimulate my interest in looking in more detail at young women who become mothers whilst in care. Firstly, in looking back over my caseload during thirteen years of working in child care, I was struck by the frequency with which young women in care became preg-nant. It appeared to me to be the norm rather than an infrequent occurrence. I had no idea whether this was a peculiarity of my caseload or my geograph-ical area or of young women in care generally. I gained a subjective impres-sion that pregnancy in young women in care was creating anxiety amongst workers and managers rather than being anticipated as a real possibility for which plans should be made. I had also gained the impression that young women were often required to move within the care system because they were pregnant and that little consideration was being given to their attachment needs at this important time. The expectation that young women in care as young as sixteen should be 'independent' has also been a cause of concern.

Over the years I have worked with families where the mother has been in care as á young person and where a child of hers has been removed and placed for adoption. I have also been the social worker for young children who have been compulsorily removed from their young mothers who themselves had been in care.

These experiences have left a deep impression on me and I have thought about whether these separations could have been prevented with better emotional support for these young mothers.

Background and evidence

There is evidence that the pregnancy rate amongst care leavers is considerably higher than that in the population at large. Biehal's study found 25% of care leavers were parents (1992). Another study of care leavers in a large county in the south found an overall lower pregnancy figure but with pockets where 40% of young women leaving care were pregnant (Clements 1994). My own study was conducted in one such pocket. In the population at large however, only about 3% of young women aged 19 and under have babies. Schofield (1994) notes that over 50% of 16 year old girls are sexually active but that the wish to become pregnant plays a relatively small part in distinguishing those who become pregnant and those who do not.

Once pregnancy has been diagnosed, the decision to continue with the pregnancy and to keep the baby is determined largely by the level of the young woman's aspirations before she becomes pregnant. The well-documented evidence that care leavers have very low expectations of pursuing a career or further education provides an explanation of why care leavers may make little effort to prevent conception and why they choose to continue with their pregnancies once diagnosed. The high profile of care leavers in almost all groups of socially disadvantaged young people has been extensively documented. Part of the reason why care leavers fare so badly is that – apart from their frequently disrupted early lives which necessitated them being in care in the first place – their time in care is often further disrupted by frequent moves. Every move is a further separation from tenuously built attachments. Compounding this disruption is the expectation that care leavers should be self-sufficient at a much earlier age than young people in the general population. Biehal's study (1992) of care leavers found that the vast majority (68%) were living independently in flats, bedsits or similar accommodation at eighteen whereas only 7% of non-care leavers had left home at eighteen.

Expecting care leavers as young as sixteen to be independent has been criticised by several workers. Stein and Carey (1986) suggest that the concept of 'interdependence' is a more helpful objective because this builds in relationships which have had previous attachments, whether to people or places. Biehal's study of care leaving mothers confirmed that they were only slightly more likely to be receiving aftercare support than their peers. Aftercare projects have been slow to recognise the numerical significance and needs of young parents – sometimes banning babies from drop-in centres, confusing the roles of child protection and support and utilising staff from youth work backgrounds who may have little rapport with young mothers.

Emotional support and attachment

The importance of attachments or the presence of significant others for physical and mental health has been widely researched. Brown and Harris' study (1978) provided evidence for 'the protective role of more enduring relationships for mental health' and Oakley's study of pregnant women revealed the effectiveness of friends in preventing birth complications (1992).

Bowlby's concept of the secure base is a helpful one when looking at emotional support:

> For not only young children, it is now clear, that human beings of all ages are found to be at their happiest and to be able to deploy their talents to best advantage when they are confident that, standing behind them, there are one or more trusted persons who will come to their aid should difficulties arise. The person trusted provides a secure base from which his (or her) companion can operate. And the more trustworthy the base the more it is taken for granted; and the more it is taken for granted, unfortunately, the more likely is its importance to be overlooked and forgotten. (Bowlby 1973: p.407)

Bowlby also highlights the paradoxical position of a self-reliant person in which independence or self-reliance is more likely to be achieved when support is available:

> The truly self-reliant person . . . proves to be by no means as independent as cultural stereotypes suppose. An essential ingredient is a capacity to rely trustingly on others when occasion demands and to know on whom it is appropriate to rely. A healthy self-reliant person is . . . at one time providing a secure base from which his companion(s) can operate; at another he is glad to rely on one or another of his companions to provide him with just such a base in return. (Bowlby 1973 p.407)

The concept of self-reliance is very significant when considering the needs of care leavers who without support are unlikely to be able to achieve mature interdependence.

Social support and mothering

The significance of social support and mothering is that there is a cyclical

148

connection between the two. The better support a mother receives during her pregnancy and neonatal phase the better it seems she will attach to her baby, or to use Winnicott's image, if she is held she will be able to hold her baby securely. The better the mother and baby are attached, the better prognosis for the future mental health of the child and the better parent that child is likely to be to her own children:

> We now have a consensus amongst scientists from a wide range of disciplines that the human capacities for love and for learning are rooted in the sensorimotor period of development, the first eighteenth months of life. The developmental significance of emotional impoverishment in infancy and the disruption of human bonds in the early years of life is documented in literature on maternal and sensory deprivation that has sobered a generation of scientists. (Fraiberg 1980)

Bowlby does not see the need for support during pregnancy and birth as a weakness – far from it: the urge to keep proximity is to be respected, valued and nurtured as making for potential strength, instead of being looked down upon, as so often hitherto as a sign of inherent weakness (quoted in Murray Parkes 1991). Bowlby shifted the conceptual framework from regarding the need for others as immature to seeing it as a valued human characteristic.

When thinking about care leavers and their babies the concept of attachment is crucial. Young women in care will have had a variety of attachment experiences. It would be unduly pessimistic to think that all had experienced poor attachments in their early years. However the inescapable fact is that all those who stay in care for more than a brief spell will have experienced at least one loss of attachment (to their family) by coming into care. Bowlby points out that 'for most individuals the bond to parents continues into adult life and affects behaviour in countless ways.' During adolescent and adult life a measure of attachment behaviour is directed not only towards persons outside the family but also towards groups and institutions other than the family. A school or college, a work group, a religious group or a political group can come to constitute for many people a subordinate attachment 'figure' (Bowlby 1969: p.207). A children's home could become the attachment 'figure' and forced separation from it can be distressing and provoke separation anxiety and anger in a young person.

Separation and dysfunction anger

It is inevitable that young people in care will have experienced at least one move or separation. The move from their family of origin is often the first of many moves within the care system. Such moves can cause the young person to feel angry. Again quoting Bowlby:

Separations, especially when prolonged or repeated have a double effect. On the one hand, anger is aroused; on the other, love is attenuated. Thus not only may angry discontented behaviour alienate the attachment figure but, within the attached, a shift can occur in the balance of feeling. Instead of strongly rooted affection laced occasionally with 'hot displeasure', such as develops in a child brought up by affectionate parents, there grows a deep-running resentment held in check only partially by anxious uncertain affection.

The most violently angry and dysfunctional responses of all, it seems probable, are elicited in children and adolescents who not only experience repeated separations but are constantly subjected to the threat of being abandoned. (1973 p.288)

Bowlby goes on to point out that anger directed at a parent is usually repressed and switched to other targets. For young people who come into care, that other target is likely to be the Social Services Department or their social worker, foster carer or residential home. It is particularly poignant when the young person's anger is displaced onto the very people or place where they want to remain, but their acting out is not tolerated and they are forced to move. This experience is likely to generate yet more anger which is likely to be displaced onto their next placement, setting in train a pattern of moves which are all too familiar.

By ignoring young people's needs for continuity of attachment and their need for emotional and social security we may be harming their ability to become a secure base for their own babies. For young women who may not have 'introjected a good enough mother' (Winnicott 1988) it becomes imperative for Social Services Departments to provide substitute 'good-enough' mothering.

The study

In the case of young mothers in care, I wanted to find answers for the following questions:

- How did they come to be in care?
- What were their experiences of moves and disruptions during their care careers?
- From whom or from where did they get their emotional support?
- What were their perceptions of the local authority's role and did they feel it was supportive?
- What was their relationships with their babies?
- What were their ideas about how things might be improved?

I interviewed five young women and three social workers involved with care leavers. The aim was to explore the adolescent's experiences of becoming mothers while still in the care of the local authority.

The mothers

I have changed all names to protect confidentiality. All the mothers and their babies were white of British descent. All five mothers had their first babies when they were seventeen years old.

Karen, aged twenty-one when I interviewed her, had been received into care on a voluntary basis at the age of thirteen. At Karen's request her baby, Beth, was accommodated for three months when she was nearly a year old. Karen has now married and has a second daughter.

Mandy, age twenty-two at the time of interview, was admitted to care at the age of twelve when she went missing from home. She was made the subject of a Care Order. She asked for her daughter, Trudie, to be accommodated when Trudie was about seven months old and subsequently Mandy asked for Trudie to be placed for adoption. Mandy has now moved away from the local area and is studying.

Emma was eighteen when I interviewed her. She was admitted to care at the age of twelve and made the subject of a Care Order. She met her present partner when her baby, Melissa, was two months old. At the time of the interview she was expecting his baby.

Becky had been admitted to care at the age of five following the death of her mother and her father's inability to cope with his children. She remained with the same foster family throughout her childhood. She left to live with her boyfriend following the birth of her first child, Dean, but returned to live with her foster carers following the birth of her second child. She was still living with them when I interviewed her at the age of twenty-one.

Dawn was eighteen at the time of interview. She had been admitted to care at the age of thirteen because of her mother's illness. She was living on her own with Lee, her young son.

Apart from Becky, whose mother died, all the other young women came into care as a result of difficulties of one kind or another with mothers and were not living with their fathers. The fathers of all four had left when the young women were between two and six. For the fifth, her father had been unable to cope with his family following the mother's death. Some contact with birth parents and siblings had been maintained although in some cases this was either infrequent or ambivalent.

Disrupted attachments

All five young women had suffered separations from one or other parent at an early age – four from their fathers and one from both parents. There had also been other separations before coming into care. Mandy had been sent to live with a variety of relatives before coming into care because of her behaviour, and one aunt, to whom she became particularly attached, died of cancer. Emma had been sent to her father for a while when she was a child but she did not like her stepmother and so left.

Once in the care system three of the young people (Karen, Mandy and Emma) experienced further moves and disruptions. Becky stayed in the same foster home throughout her time in care from the age of five. Dawn stayed in the same foster home from the age of thirteen until she left at seventeen when she experienced a further loss from the death of her foster mother. She did not get on so well with the foster sister who took over her care.

For Mandy, Emma and Karen there were many moves. Foster placements were attempted but did not work and they all found themselves in children's homes which they preferred. Emma and Karen didn't 'get on' in their foster homes while Mandy found her's uncomfortable because she thought the foster parents were 'doing it for the money'. She could not relax and 'just wanted to get out'.

On the other hand children's homes were liked by the three girls who went to live in them:

It was brilliant in the kid's home – because the staff were on site you could walk out of your bedroom in your nightie, and go and sit in there with everybody. They'd make you a cup of tea and it wasn't like there's a social worker in her office.

When Mandy left she felt as though she had been 'dumped' out of the children's home. She was glad to leave because of another resident but 'I didn't want to leave; I got into a fight with another resident, then got sick of it, wanted to move in the end but I didn't want to leave the staff'. As Mandy put it:

At least at (children's home) if you were down, staff would know. One of them could come up and knock on your bedroom door and have a chat and that would help and even though there were more children there, I got more affection and more of what I needed there than with (foster carers).

She felt bitterly disappointed about having to leave because of staffing problems and expressed her anger at this broken attachment: 'I didn't visit (children's home) after I left. It wasn't fair that I had to go and others stayed.'

Emma too had to leave the children's home very abruptly. She had found

152

the staff 'brilliant'. She was moved from the children's home because of staffing problems. When she returned to the home there was 'a massive row'. Emma was given an ultimatum either to settle down or to go. She expressed her anger towards the rejection by the children's home by rejecting it and told the staff she would go.

Both Mandy and Emma became pregnant shortly after leaving the children's home. Karen was already pregnant when she left but did not realise until she was over four months pregnant, although she claims that the staff all knew. All three girls were pregnant and living independently in bedsits at sixteen years of age. Dawn, too, became pregnant shortly after she had left her foster home.

Emotional support and attachments in care

For Becky, her foster home clearly provided her with a secure base and she made strong attachments to her foster parents and their children. She was able to leave for a while and return with her children.

Dawn too had a stable period of four years in the same home and although she left at seventeen as a result of difficulties with her foster sister she often returned and kept in contact with the foster carers and their other foster children. By the time Dawn had her baby she had undergone a reconciliation with her father and stepmother – her son providing the focus of their positive interest. An additional factor in her stability was the presence of her sister in the same town. This sister accompanied Dawn at the birth of her son. Dawn was also able to use her social worker 'for money and talking' and she had a positive view of Social Services: 'Social Services couldn't do more, be in care if you want the help; I wouldn't have been able to do it without the Social Services.' Thus Dawn had several supportive adults with whom she had some sort of attachment relationship.

The three young women who had been moved out of children's homes at an early point had to rely mostly on their social workers for support. Their experiences were more varied and ambivalent.

Emma explained that she had rows with her social worker but she wanted him to continue with her because he had been her sister's social worker too. She trusted him and he knew the family. This young woman was also effective in engaging other members of staff and built up a very good relationship with her social worker's clerk. If Emma's social worker wasn't there, she said: 'I would pop in and tell (clerk) after my scan and after the baby was born. I didn't go to Social Services any more after she left. I still phone her sometimes at the place where she works now.'

In this case the arrangement established to provide Emma with her money, enabled her to visit the office frequently without having to have a 'problem'. This provided her with an opportunity to gain support from someone of her choice. It is unlikely that this sort of support can be planned but it was of great significance to Emma and it is important for agencies to tolerate and encourage these sorts of spontaneous attachments. Emma also had a sister to whom she could turn.

For both Karen and Mandy their experiences with social workers were less successful. Karen had very strong views of her own and found herself in conflict with her social worker. She was able, with the help of a friend, to ask for a change. However, she found the experience of going to see her social worker and being told she was out, to be rejecting. It also made her feel angry: 'You visit your social worker and you are told they're out at the moment would you like to see the clerk? And you think Christ what good is that to me now, and you have to wait two or three days or come back later, you don't always need someone later.' Karen's inability to wait no doubt reflected a repetition of earlier experiences with her father who she described as having 'abandoned' her as a child and she remembered waiting for hours for failed visits.

Karen had difficulties in talking to the clerk if her social worker was out because she was worried about 'everyone knowing your business'. She had 'sat down and cried' when she visited the office and there was no one there. Karen found it 'awkward' if she had to go to the same person for everything. She would ask for money and then be asked 'are you beating up that baby?'

Karen was highlighting the difficulty of the dual role of field workers in both aftercare and child protection. Karen felt keenly the difference in status between herself and social workers.

She frequently referred to her feelings of incompetence in relation to other people, especially social workers; feelings perhaps stemming from her earlier experiences with her own mother who 'could do everything' and who also worked with children. Karen did however speak highly of a family support worker provided by Social Services with whom she could 'sit and have a chat and a fag' and who 'really helped her'.

Karen's main form of emotional support was a friend, about ten years older, another lone parent who she met whilst she was pregnant and living on her own. Her friend was like: 'a big kid, a mum, a big sister, a best of mates, a bit of everything. I'd have been stuck without her, been at Social Services door all the time'. This was the person Karen chose to have with her at Beth's birth.

Of the five mothers Mandy had the greatest difficulty finding any support. She did not find any sustaining support following her rejection from the children's home: 'I lost faith in Social Services after I left (the home).' She chose as a support her boyfriend and desperately wanted to move in with him so that she could leave the foster home which she intensely disliked. She was unable to trust anyone enough to tell them when her boyfriend began to be violent towards her and their baby. Because her relationship with social workers had revolved around court hearings, meetings and reviews, she thought that she: 'had to be good in front of social workers. Being beaten up by a complete psychopath was not one of the good reports you should be giving them'.

Mandy had sufficient insight to understand how this inability to trust might have come about:

I always had to rely on me, I always tried not to turn to people because if I turned to my mum she was always too busy with the other children, trying to get some money to feed and clothe us. When I've wanted to turn to someone it's been 'not now, I'm busy'. I've always felt you had to deal with things yourself. I found Social Services really unapproachable.

Whilst the other young women appeared to have managed some level of reconciliation with their families – assisted often by the arrival of their babies, there had been no real rapprochement between Mandy and her mother. Neither Mandy nor Karen had sisters to turn to, whereas both Dawn and Emma had derived support from their older sisters and had them present at the births of their babies.

The mothers and their babies

In the study, I wanted to gain some sense of whether the support given to these young mothers during their pregnancies had helped or not in their early relationships with their babies. The most significant experiences for most mothers is of course the quality of their own parenting from birth and throughout their lives. Given that pregnancy is a time when attachment needs are particularly acute and given that young women in care are unlikely to be able to turn to their own mothers for support in the way that most women do, it is important for local authorities to know whether their services are assisting or not.

Apart from Becky, whose substitute mothering had been very adequate, all the young people I talked to, wanted to give their babies better experiences than they had had. 'I thought maybe I can put it right with this baby' said one of the mothers. They all expressed feelings of love and possession when their babies were born. This feeling of possessiveness was increased by their own sense of not having anything or anybody else: 'I've got something of my very own that I can love. I thought me and this baby could go and combat the world and nothing would get us.'

Even though Emma's baby was 'the spit' of the father whom Emma intensely disliked she: 'didn't hate her; I thought I would, I thought to myself "I don't love you". Then I looked at her and thought "I do love you really, you're mine" and that's the way I looked at it. She was just mine and no-one else's'.

All the young women spoke of this strong attachment to their babies when they were first born. However, for all except Becky it was not plain sailing. Becky had a 'wonderful' baby and 'was very sure of what she was doing and did not need help'. However she knew she could call on her foster family if necessary and she would have worried if she was on her own.

For two of the mothers all did not go well in the baby's early life. Dawn's baby had to spend three weeks in a distant hospital shortly after birth. Because she nearly lost her baby she 'loved him more' but she felt very much on her own in a strange city and would have 'liked someone then' to support her.

Emma's baby was admitted to hospital at six weeks with gastric problems and Emma also had post-natal depression. She was able to talk to her sister who had also experienced post-natal depression and would have 'cracked up' if she had not been able to talk about it. Mandy also suffered from periods of depression and she 'sat holding Trudie and crying', becoming more and more desperate about her boyfriend but not feeling she could get help from either her mother or Social Services.

Both Dawn and Emma found support which they valued. For Dawn it came from a combination of her ex-foster family and her own family. Emma met her present partner when her baby was two months old. He and her family plus a social worker whom she trusted combined to provide her with the support she needed even though her little girl is 'a naughty little cow'. Dawn and Emma both found it easier as their babies got older.

Karen and Mandy on the other hand had found it harder as the children grew older. By two months Karen's baby, Beth, was a 'horrible little baby' especially during the night when Karen 'hated her'. Respite care and child-minding proved insufficient for Karen and when her baby was nearly a year old she asked for her to be accommodated. Karen had three months without Beth which she described as 'heaven' and during this time she met her husband. After Beth returned Karen 'didn't feel nasty towards her' but before she went, Karen 'used to want to shake her'. Her new relationship was enough to sustain her from then on. Although this period of accommodation for Beth could be considered negatively, it seemed that Social Services did come up with the support that Karen needed at that time. The Social Services provided a good supplementary attachment experience for her baby daughter who continues to go to a nursery run by the same foster carer with whom she was accommodated.

For Mandy the unhappy experiences of her earlier and present life became insurmountable. Earlier experiences of rejection and separation from her mother, father, aunt and uncle and the children's home contributed to her inability to trust anyone. As a child she felt, in the words of Klein (1987), that 'good things are being withheld, that good people have gone away'. Such feelings prevented her from running the risk of asking for help in case she suffered further rebuffs. She split off her needy side and did not permit this to be shown to her social worker. There was little positive to hold on to for Mandy and eventually she began to see herself as being a bad mother, offering Trudie nothing more than a repetition of her own bad life experiences. She was determined not to inflict this onto her own child. When Trudie was less than a year old Mandy asked for her to be accommodated and eventually adopted.

The mothers' views of the support services varied according to their own experiences of the support which they had received. However, they were unanimous in their view that support was of great importance. Becky summed it up, saying:

It's a crucial part – knowing someone's there. If you've got no-one it's bound to affect the way you feel about your baby if you've got no-one there and you're having a horrible pregnancy, chances are you're going to end up disliking being pregnant, disliking having that baby and it's only going to cause dislike for the child. When you've got no-one things seem ten times worse.

The two mothers who had had less good experiences with Social Services thought young people should be able to stay in children's homes when they became pregnant rather than having to move out on their own. The idea of help from people who had been in the same situation came up several times. Mandy suggested young women should be provided with:

a chance to meet people in similar circumstances who they can talk to at the same level; a sort of meeting point or café where there would be older people – about twenty-two to twenty-five – not social workers but people with a bit of experience who aren't going to patronise; people to turn to – maybe volunteer people. You need things to do to occupy your mind and things involving the children and you need to remind them to go, even though you haven't heard from them. Two months later, go and remind them, go and get them by car; don't wait for them to come to you.

Karen suggested 'befrienders' who had nothing to do with social workers and she particularly emphasised the need for someone she could phone at any time:

But not if it's their job, someone who doesn't have other clients, someone you can say whatever you like to; not people who'll have a go or look down at you.

Three young women, who had not been in foster homes, thought that they themselves could become just such a support for other younger women. They thought that they would be well suited to help other young mothers because 'they had been there'.

It was clear that several of the young women were very aware of the difference in status between themselves and social workers.

You get some smarmy little git sitting there saying 'I know how you feel dear' and you think 'you don't'. They sit there and they've got their nice little family and their nine to five job and their car and they don't have to worry about money, not half as much as the rest of us.

It is unlikely that a young person will be able to turn for help from someone about whom she has such negative feelings. The social worker's role if she suspects her client is feeling oppressed, is to mobilize other parts of the supportive network to help the young person.

Attachment, resilience and reflection

The contrasting experiences of Becky and Mandy illustrate nicely the contrasting abilities of children to take advantage of love and support. Becky suffered serious losses as a child but a substitute family provided very successful continuous compensatory attachments and she was able to use her foster family as a secure base – leaving for a while and then returning with her own children. Mandy on the other hand was abandoned by her father at a very early age and she also felt her mother was always boo busy for her. She went to live with her aunt to whom she became very attached but she died. Within the care system Mandy was forced to move out of a children's home where she felt attached and eventually chose as her support a violent boyfriend. Because of this series of rejections she was unable to use the albeit inadequate support from Social Services, anticipating rebuffs if she confided in the worker. She was the only interviewee whose child is no longer with her.

There are many chances for compensatory attachments to be made. Bowlby describes the child as having:

an array of pathways potentially open to him, the one along which he will in fact proceed being determined at every moment by the interaction of the individual as he now is with the environment in which he happens to be.

Children who have insensitive, unresponsive, neglectful or rejecting parents are likely to develop along a deviant pathway which is in some degree incompatible with mental health and which renders them vulnerable to breakdown, should they meet with seriously adverse events.

Bowlby's view is not altogether pessimistic. He suggests that changes in the way a child is treated can shift the pathway in a more or less favourable direction and: 'although the capacity for developmental change diminishes with age change continues throughout the life cycle so that changes for better or worse are always possible'. (Bowlby 1988 p.136)

This seems to be an important message for those working with young people in care to prevent them from becoming unduly pessimistic or becoming too fixated on the idea of intergenerational transmission of deprivation. Such a message could also act as a stimulus to those planning the care system to provide conditions where attachments are facilitated for a new generation of babies born to those in care – its grandchildren.

In Mandy's case, moves whilst in care served to intensify her distrust of Social Services. They could have been prevented. Another chance for support occurred when she had her baby and began to feel overwhelmingly that she was providing a life style no better for her baby than she had experienced herself.

More recent work based upon attachment theory is attempting to disentangle the elements which prevent the intergenerational transmission of parenting breakdown. How is it that some children are more resilient to emotional problems in adulthood than others in the face of childhood adversity? What can we do to create resilience? Fonagy concludes that 'secure attachment is a legitimate goal of intervention'. His theory is that the 'reflective-self function' in the mother enables her to reflect on the infant's mental state by entering into his or her mental world and this ability acts as a protective process. The ability of the infant then to develop the 'reflective-self function' 'allows for the modification of unhelpful internal working models of relationships through encounters with new significant figures, it equips the individual with ballast, a self-righting capacity' (Fonagy 1994). The child is able to build up an internal working model of empathic responses which he or she can draw upon when facing adversity.

Selma Fraiberg offers a model of intervention with mothers and babies which she calls 'unconventional therapy' and 'developmental guidance' and which she argues, is likely to facilitate the development of reflective-self function:

> The therapeutic work for the mother is one of listening, observing, giving permission to feel and to remember that which can be remembered, examining the past in the present, undoing the painful effects of the past, giving hope and the prospects of new solutions to old problems. The therapeutic work for the baby is one in which the mother is helped to recognise the baby as a symbol of her abandoned self to find pathways to understanding the sorrows of early childhood, to find pathways of feeling which can unite the mother with her baby in hope instead of futility. (Fraiberg 1980 p.55)

The concept that attachments can be fortified at different stages of a child's path through life, not only with his or her family but whilst in care and setting up his or her own families, offers an optimistic focus for child care workers.

The social worker as attachment broker

In some cases a social worker might become an attachment figure for a young person in care or certainly one of a number of attachments. In the present study some of the young women found that their social workers were supportive. These were the young people who had significant others to turn to as well, including sisters, foster carers or remnants of birth families. Downes (1992) helps to clarify the role of social workers in her study of fostering older adolescents. Her concepts, however, can be applied in a wider context of care. She sees the role of the social worker focusing on the 'care giving network' rather than being the care giver herself. The social worker can be the 'secure base' for the foster carers or other carers of the young person, someone to whom they can express their negative feelings about the young person:

> The aim is to enable an angry foster parent to recover a more reflective stance. An indication that this point has been reached is that they are able to begin to think the incident through from the stance of the adolescent, and to think about the impact that each has had on the other.

There are parallels here with Fonagy's thesis that if parents can focus on the mental world of the child then their children can be helped to become more resilient. With foster carers, the social worker's task is to enable them to reflect upon the adolescent's mental world. Not only does this enable the foster carer to become more resilient, but the young person too is witness to a more reflective stance which may provide them with a model for the future. The social worker may need to perform this function for various strands of the caring network – birth family, foster carers and their own children, residential workers, other residents, other professionals and voluntary agencies. Downes suggests that the social worker is the secure base from which the care-giving network can work effectively with the adolescent.

Attachment theory and practice

A sizeable proportion of young people in care are likely to become mothers. When services are planned the special needs of this group should be recognised. Previous discussion has focused on the significance of preserving attachments for young people in care generally, but particularly for young mothers, in order to enhance their capabilities as parents. Yet often young pregnant women experience more, rather than fewer, separations.

Because attachment is sometimes confused with dependency, I suspect that there can be a reluctance on the part of an organisation to value or even acknowledge that social workers or residential workers, let alone clerks, can become 'attachment figures' for young people. It may seem easier to move young people or change their worker than to acknowledge their attachment but this denies the anger or depression which will eventually erupt somewhere else in the system. Moving is seen as the solution to an immediate crisis but it creates a new crisis for the child and carers in the next placement. If carers could become familiar with the concept of displaced anger following separation they might be relieved of the sense of persecution and responsibility they feel when young people act out in placement.

By denying the existence of attachments, both those of young people as well as those of workers and carers, maintaining contact once children move is seen as unnecessary. Berridge and Cleaver's study of foster home breakdowns provides strong evidence that even after disruption, contact should be encouraged. They found that social workers were often punitive towards foster carers and that they viewed 'care careers as a set of discrete packages rather than an integrated experience' (Berridge and Cleaver 1987 p.167). In the way that keeping contact with birth families is now accepted as essential to a child's identity and self esteem, keeping contact with other significant attachment experiences in substitute care needs to be given a heightened emphasis.

The concepts of attachment could be incorporated in planning leaving care and after care provision, such plans should build on a young person's existing support networks and relationships and not seek to replace them. For many young people, keeping the same social worker or remaining in the same community home or foster home would be preferable to a change. Independence units in children's homes are a good way of maintaining attachments whilst still allowing for increased independence.

Although the concept of 'a family for life' has gained some recognition, young people are often prevented from staying on in foster homes beyond the age of eighteen because of the failure of local authorities to make suitable financial provision for foster care. This often occurs even when both the young person and the foster carers do not want to break their relationship. In a similar vein it is important for a young person's file not to be closed automatically at eighteen but, if feasible, for the file to remain on the caseload of the same social worker. The local authority has a duty to provide advice and assistance up to the age of twenty-one. Young people often do return to see their social workers, sometimes years later. They should feel entitled to return to the same social worker rather than have to go through a duty system. To see a familiar face is important for the young person. It can be rewarding for the social worker (who can also become attached).

We have known for many years about early attachment experiences affecting subsequent mothering; that additional losses, moves and separations compound earlier poor attachment experiences; that good subsequent emotional support and attachment can ameliorate poor prior experiences; and that pregnancy and birth are times of particular vulnerability and need for emotional support and dependence on attachment figures. We need to remind ourselves of the particular vulnerability of the young people who have babies and for whom we care. The care and support normally provided by families has to be provided by Social Services workers. The opportunity exists at this time to either exacerbate or ameliorate the young women's pre-existing emotional difficulties. It is a time when preventative services can be very effective in terms of diminishing the cost of future family breakdown and suffering. This support is unlikely to be provided by one person. It needs to be flexible and varied to take into account the varied past experiences and present circumstances of the young mothers.

It is important for us to ensure that we are not unconsciously punishing our young care leavers for becoming pregnant and that by responding empathically to the needs of these young women we may give them a model of support and holding which well enable them to support and hold their babies.

References

Berridge, D., and Cleaver, H. (1987) *Foster Home Breakdown* Oxford: Blackwell.

Biehal, N., Clayden, J., Stein, M., and Wade, J. (1992) *Prepared for Living?* Leeds: Leeds University Press.

Bowlby, J. (1969) *Attachment and Loss Vol. 1 Attachment*, London: Hogarth Press.

Bowlby, J. (1973) *Attachment & Loss Vol. 2 Separation: Anxiety and Anger* Harmondsworth: Penguin.

Bowlby, J. (1988) *A Secure Base* London: Routledge.

Brown, G. W. & Harris, T. (1978) *The Social Origins of Depression* London: Tavistock Publications.

Clements, A., and Smith, L. (1994) *Leaving Care Report* (Draft) Essex County Council Research and Inspection Section.

Dobson, R.(1994) 'Rare Breed' *Community Care* 18 August: 22.

Downes, C. (1992) *Separation Revisited* Aldershot: Ashgate.

Fonagy, P., Steele, M., Steele, H., Higgitt, A., Target, M., (1994) 'The Theory and Practice of Resilience' *J. Child Psychology and Psychiatry* Vol. 35 pp.231–257.

Fraiberg, S. (ed) 1980 *Clinical Studies in Infant Mental Health* London: Tavistock Publications.

Klein, J. (1987) *Our Need for Others and its Roots in Infancy* London: Tavistock.

Oakley, A. (1992) *Social Support and Motherhood* Oxford: Blackwell.

Schofield, G. (1994) *The Youngest Mothers* Aldershot: Avebury.

Stein, M. & Carey, K. (1986) *Leaving Care* Oxford: Blackwell.

Winnicott, D. (1988) *Babies and their Mothers* London: Free Association Books.

Subject index

adaptive responses 14–15, 63–65
adoption 131–135, 137, 141
adversity 1–2, 23–24
affectional bonds 15
after care support 161
amae 60, 68
ambivalent attachments 10–12, 15, 22
anxiety 6–8, 10–14, 112
anxious attachments 10–13, 23
arousal–relaxation cycle 40–42, 55
assessments 16–18, 24, 46–47, 50
attachment behaviour 6–7, 14–15, 38, 59, 149
attachment broker 150–160
attachment classification system 9–14, 21–22
attachment needs 147–162
attachment theory, definition of 3–4
avoidant attachments 12–13, 15, 21, 69–70

bereavement 61
breakdown rates in child placements 133

care leavers 146–162
child abuse 18–35, 87–89, 131
child development 115
child placements 129
child protection 18–35
child protection conference 29–30
Children Act 1989 19, 24–25, 41, 44,
 47, 101, 105, 136, 138, 142
children's rights 117, 129
clean breaks 103, 130, 132
Cleveland Inquiry 19, 97
cognitive deficits 37
compulsive self-reliance 12, 15, 148
conflict 8, 11, 14
contact centre 108–112
contact, parent–child 16, 25, 101–127, 142
cultural contexts 3–4, 59–76
cultural imperialism 65
cultural norms 61
cultural psychology 60, 62
cultural relativism 59–76

defense mechanisms 7–8, 14–15
depression 12, 30, 97, 156
developmental needs 47, 51
developmental psychology 1, 3, 15
disorganised attachments 13, 22
disrupted attachments 152–153
disruption 133
divorce 101–112

ecological approach 71–72, 76
emotional abuse 29, 33, 51, 87–89, 90–91
emotional neglect 37
emotional support 148, 153, 161
empathy 40, 159
eye contact 60–62